EXPLORATIONS IN LOCAL AND

REGIONAL HISTORY

Centre for Regional and Local History, University of Hertfordshire
and
Centre for English Local History, University of Leicester

SERIES EDITORS: KATRINA NAVICKAS AND RICHARD JONES

FARMERS, CONSUMERS, INNOVATORS

The world of Joan Thirsk

EDITED BY RICHARD JONES
AND CHRISTOPHER DYER

UNIVERSITY OF HERTFORDSHIRE PRESS

Explorations in Local and Regional History
Volume 8

First published in Great Britain in 2016 by
University of Hertfordshire Press
College Lane
Hatfield
Hertfordshire
AL10 9AB

British Library Cataloguing in Publication Data
A catalogue record for this book is available from the British Library

ISBN 978-1-909291-56-0

Design by Arthouse Publishing Solutions Ltd
Printed in Great Britain by Henry Ling Ltd, Dorchester

Contents

Figures

Tables

Contributors

JAMES BOWEN is a Postdoctoral Research Associate based at the Department of Geography and Planning, the School of Environmental Sciences, University of Liverpool. He completed a PhD at Lancaster University entitled 'The governance and management of common land in Shropshire between the sixteenth and nineteenth centuries', and held the Economic History Society's Tawney Fellowship in 2012–13.

JOHN BROAD was one of Joan Thirsk's first students when she went to Oxford. He taught Economic and Social History at London Metropolitan University and its predecessors for most of his working life, and is now attached to the Cambridge Group for the History of Population and Social Structure, where he is researching the Land Tax and completing projects on Rural Housing and Social Structure.

JOHN CHARTRES is Emeritus Professor of Social and Economic History at the University of Leeds. He is a former President of the British Agricultural History Society. He was one of Joan Thirsk's very first undergraduate students at Oxford and was supervised by her for his DPhil. With David Hey he edited Joan's first festschrift in 1990.

MARK DAWSON received his doctorate from the University of Nottingham in 2007. He works in the computer industry but continues to research and write about the history of food and drink and is on the committee of the Leeds Food History Symposium.

CHRISTOPHER DYER is Emeritus Professor of History at the University of Leicester. His research covers social and economic history, archaeology and the study of the landscape, in the middle ages in England. His most recent book was *A Country Merchant* (2012) and he is now writing a book on peasant farming.

DAVID HEY was Emeritus Professor of Local and Family History and an Honorary Doctor of Letters at the University of Sheffield. He was President of the British

Association for Local History, Chairman of the British Record Society, and a Council Member of the Marc Fitch Fund. In 1971 Joan Thirsk was the External Examiner for his PhD thesis at Leicester.

RICHARD HOYLE was the last of Joan Thirsk's doctoral students at Oxford. After a long period as Professor of Rural History at Reading, he is now Professor of Local and Regional History at the University of London and Director and General Editor of VCH. He continues to edit *Agricultural History Review*.

RICHARD JONES is Senior Lecturer in Landscape History in the Centre for English Local History at Leicester University. He has published on the origins of English rural settlements, place-naming and manure. He is currently exploring the presence, behaviour and characteristics of water in the English landscape past and present.

CRAIG MULDREW'S research focuses on the economic and social role of trust in the development of the market economy in England between 1550 and 1800, and the living standards and work of agricultural labourers in the early modern English economy.

SUSAN NORTH is Curator of Fashion 1550–1800 at the Victoria and Albert Museum, and has co-authored several Museum publications relating to early modern dress. Susan has an MA in the history of dress from the Courtauld Institute and a PhD from Queen Mary, University of London.

JON STOBART is Professor of History at Manchester Metropolitan University. His research interests cover a range of themes within retail and consumption history in eighteenth-century England. Most recently, Jon's work has centred on the processes of supply and practices of consumption English within country houses, culminating in a monograph entitled *Consumption and the Country House* (2016).

NICOLA WHYTE lectures on landscape and early modern social history in the Department of History, University of Exeter. Her research interests revolve around the constitution of everyday landscapes in the past with particular reference to understanding social relations, situated knowledge and memory practices. She is currently working on her next book on landscape, place and dwelling in early modern England and Wales.

TOM WILLIAMSON is Professor of Landscape History at the University of East Anglia and has written widely on landscape history, historical ecology and the history of landscape design. His books include *Shaping medieval landscapes* (2003), *Environment, society and landscape in early medieval England* (2013) and, with Tracey Partida and Rob Liddiard, *Champion: the making and unmaking of English Midland landscapes* (2013).

Series Editors' Preface

Explorations in Local and Regional History continues the series of 'Occasional Papers' of the University of Leicester's Department (now Centre) for English Local History, started in 1952. This succeeding series is published by the University of Hertfordshire Press with the Centre for Regional and Local History Research and the University of Leicester.

Explorations in Local and Regional History has three distinctive aims. First, the series seeks to open up new directions, prompt analysis of new sources and develop innovative methodologies in local and regional history. The series follows the fine tradition set by the universities of Leicester and Hertfordshire in empirical research into communities, place, landscape, demography, and social and economic change from the medieval era to the present day. But it also seeks new ways to reinvigorate the significance of local and regional history in the twenty-first century. Though local and regional history can be bounded physically by geography, it is not bounded by connections and networks that stretch over time and space. Local history drills down to find the meaning of place at all levels, from the micro to the global. We encourage both detailed studies of localities in Britain and Europe as well as comparative and more theoretical approaches.

The second aim of the series is to provide an outlet for mid-length studies in between research articles and full-length books, generally within the range of 40,000 to 60,000 words. Such works are hard to place with existing publishers, so our series offers a space for detailed, yet quicker to read, studies than standard monographs. We encourage innovative work from researchers at the start of their careers as well as from more established scholars.

Third, we hope this series is of interest to both academics and students, but also to researchers outside universities. Local heritage is a vital part of today's society and government: applied local history research enables community building through the commemoration of place, informs policies regarding conservation of both the built and natural environment, and of course helps to promote towns and regions for tourism. This series aims to provide historical context for these uses of heritage.

Richard Jones, University of Leicester
Katrina Navickas, University of Hertfordshire

Preface and acknowledgements

This book began with a conference held at the University of Leicester on 20 September 2014, almost a year after the death of Joan Thirsk. The event was attended by 120 people. It was organised with help from the University of Leicester, the Friends of the Centre for English Local History, the Agricultural History Society and the Economic History Society. Valuable help and support came from Lucy Byrne, Susan Kilby, Robert Mee, Ann Stones and Susannah Wade-Martins. Andy Hopper and Jane Whittle acted as chairs.

A well-attended memorial meeting had been held in London earlier in the year, so our event at Leicester (where Joan Thirsk had been a member of staff for 14 years) was designed instead to honour a great historian by examining her legacy as it influenced historical thinking in the twenty-first century. Participants were urged to make reference to Joan's work, but not to look back. They were expected to identify the relevance of her thinking and writing at the present time, and to show in their new research how they had been influenced and inspired by her. Some of the speakers are scholars who had known Joan, and as students had been taught and supervised by her; others were younger people who had not met her, but knew of her ideas from her publications.

We should like to thank all our contributors for accepting to deliver papers; for so willingly agreeing to turn these into the chapters that follow; and for following our brief so closely. Both individually and collectively they cover much ground. Readers familiar with the full scope of Joan's work will note, however, the absence of some important historical themes that she helped to pioneer and develop. Such subjects as new crops, alternative agriculture, horses, inheritance customs, books about farming and domestic management could all have been revisited because they all still attract the attention of researchers, however the length of the day at the conference, and the number of pages of this book are limited. But Joan had much to say of farmers, innovators and consumers in particular. As a consequence of her work, we got to know them. And as our contributors show, they remain people of interest of whom much can and still needs to be said.

1

Joan Thirsk at Leicester

CHRISTOPHER DYER

Most of Joan Thirsk's publications appeared when she was at Oxford, holding the post of Reader in Economic History (1965–83), or after her retirement when she was writing from her home near Tonbridge in Kent. It was however during her 14 years at Leicester (1951–65) that she developed her skills as an agrarian historian, published some important works and did much of the preparatory thinking which led to the achievements of her later years.

Before enquiring into the importance of her time in Leicester, we must ask how she chose to pursue a career in history, and why she came to work on agrarian history. As is often the case, events and chance played as much a part as deliberate intention.

Joan Watkins was born in 1922 into a north London family which was not academic. Her mother had worked as a dressmaker, and her father, who had trained as a leather worker, after the First World War became the steward of a club in the west end. They encouraged their daughter, and she was able to attend the prestigious Camden School. There she enjoyed the history lessons given by Iris Hansen, and also by Miss Bell who had been a student at the London School of Economics (LSE) and was one of a number of young women who were attracted to economic history in the early 1900s. Joan read biographies and historical novels relating to the sixteenth and seventeenth centuries, as the history of people had an appeal for her, rather than the impersonal trends found in the conventional history syllabus. Her talent for modern languages gained her a scholarship from the London County Council (LCC) to spend three months in German-speaking Switzerland during the summer holidays of 1939, from which she had to return hastily after the declaration of war on 3 September. She was drawn to languages as her main subject, and spent two years in 1939–41 at Camden School, not in its premises in Kentish Town but relocated to the east midlands, successively at Uppingham, Grantham and Stamford to avoid bombing.[1]

---

1. On her earlier life, J. Thirsk, 'Nature versus nurture', *History Workshop Journal*, 47 (1991), pp. 273–7; J. Thirsk, *Bletchley Park: an inmate's story* (Hadlow, 2008), pp. 57–8; letters and autobiographical writings by Joan Thirsk, provided by her husband Jimmy Thirsk; see also C. Dyer and P. Slack, 'Irene Joan Thirsk 1922–2013', *Biographical memoirs of Fellows of the British Academy*, 14 (2015), pp. 573–96.

In 1941–2, she was taking the first year of a modern languages degree, in German and French, at Westfield College. Again, she was evacuated from London to the safety of St Peter's Hall (now a College) at Oxford. Perhaps it was in Oxford that her conversion to history began, as she would have met history students, for example at meetings of the Labour Club. At the end of the first year of her degree she was given the choice of either completing her degree, after which she would be expected to take up school teaching, or to do war work. She took the second option, enlisted in the Auxiliary Territorial Service (ATS) and was invited to join the Intelligence Corps, where her knowledge of German could be used. After a period of training she found herself at Bletchley Park as part of a dedicated community who were decoding enemy radio messages and interpreting them. Joan's work as part of a team in the 'fusion room' was mainly concerned with plotting the location of German military units across Europe and North Africa. Again she came into contact with historians, and in her spare time read some history, in particular the Penguin edition of Tawney's *Religion and the Rise of Capitalism*. Here was a book about a period in which she already had an interest and which connected religion with social and economic history, written from a philosophical and political perspective with which she sympathised. Joan became engaged in the intense political discussions among the Bletchley community as history unfolded before their eyes.[2]

At the end of the war, Joan married Jimmy Thirsk, a librarian who she had met at Bletchley, where he worked in hut 6, and returned to Westfield to complete her degree, but now the subject was history. She explained the change in later years in typically practical terms: it was not feasible to spend time familiarising herself with the German spoken language in the midst of devastation. But her experiences during the war must have been a factor. In her two years of undergraduate history she was stimulated by the teaching at Westfield, gained a first class degree, and was given funding for a doctorate. Searching for a subject and supervisor brought her into contact with the LSE and she was recruited to work on a PhD, supervised by R.H. Tawney, on the sale of delinquents' land in the 1640s and 1650s; that is, the transfer of land that had belonged to Royalists, the Crown and the Church, and policy towards that land after 1660.[3] Her time at Bletchley had prepared her well for historical research, as she had developed the skill of extracting meaning from terse and fragmentary evidence. She completed her thesis in three years (1947–50), and then held a temporary post as an assistant lecturer in sociology at the LSE. By 1951 Joan Thirsk had become an historian of the early modern period with a connection to the social sciences, but without a specialised field.

2.   Thirsk, 'Nature versus nurture'; Thirsk, *Bletchley Park*, pp. 57–8.

3.   J. Chartres, James Thirsk and J. Robinson, 'Joan Thirsk, FBA, 1922–2013', *Agricultural History Review*, 62 (2014), p. 51; J. Thirsk, 'The sale of delinquents' estates during the Interregnum and the land settlement at the Restoration', PhD thesis (London, 1950).

How and why did she become an agrarian historian? Her urban upbringing had given her little first-hand experience of the countryside apart from cycling expeditions when her school was exiled to the east midlands. She was familiar with the research, published in the first half of the twentieth century, into medieval and early modern agriculture and rural society, but her thesis had been about the transfer of land rather than its cultivation or management. When W.G. Hoskins of the University College of Leicester, who was embarking on the revival of the *Victoria County History* (VCH) of Leicestershire, asked Tawney about a possible author for a chapter on modern agriculture, he recommended Joan. That first contact with Leicester was renewed in 1951 when Hoskins obtained funding from a special grant created by the University Grants Committee to promote research into economic history. Hoskins in his application put forward (in 1950) a grand scheme to fund research into land-use, population and agriculture, with special attention to regional variations, for the period 450–1800, beginning with a study of Lincolnshire.[4] The money was made available, and Joan Thirsk was appointed as a Senior Research Fellow in the Department of English Local History; her post was known unofficially in Leicester as the 'Agrarian Fellowship'.

Leicester was an ideal place to acquire expertise in agrarian history. The starting point for her work on Lincolnshire had to be the numerous probate inventories in the archives of the diocese. Hoskins had pioneered the study of these documents, with their details of crops and livestock listed after the death of a farmer. He had contributed essays about farming in Leicestershire as a whole, and detailed studies of individual villages.[5] Joan was advised by Hoskins, but he was her Leicester colleague for only a few months, as he took up a new post as Reader in Economic History at Oxford early in 1952. The leadership of the Department of English Local History passed to H.P.R. Finberg, who like Hoskins had worked on Devon, but his specialism also was agricultural history and Joan received much encouragement from a knowledgeable supporter.

Joan completed the first instalment of the Lincolnshire project in a year, which was published in 1953 as an Occasional Paper of the Leicester department under the title *Fenland Farming in the Sixteenth Century.*[6] This had the same comprehensive agenda that Hoskins had proposed in his bid for funding, as it dealt with population, settlements and the use of land and farming practices, basing its findings on probate inventories and documents in the Public Records office dealing with drainage improvements. Contemporaries said that the men of the fens

4.   University of Leicester Centre for English Local History, HPR Finberg papers (hereafter Finberg papers) FIN/8/2/4/22b (typescript by W.G. Hoskins).

5.   For example, W.G. Hoskins, 'The Leicestershire farmer in the sixteenth century', *Transactions of the Leicestershire Archaeological Society*, 22 (1944–5), pp. 33–94; W.G. Hoskins, 'A short history of Galby and Frisby', *Transactions of the Leicestershire Archaeological Society*, 22 (1944–5), pp. 173–210.

6.   J. Thirsk, *Fenland farming in the sixteenth century*, University of Leicester Department of English Local History Occasional paper, 3 (Leicester, 1953).

were a special breed of people, whose character was formed from battling against the adverse environment. Joan found a very successful farming system, in which prosperous yeomen could benefit from the abundant resources of their country.

Finberg encouraged and supported the progress of *Fenland Farming*, using his expertise as a former printer to ensure that it was well produced, and he persuaded Tawney to write an introduction. After much correspondence between the two Leicester colleagues about the publication he agreed to call her 'Joan' rather than 'Mrs Thirsk'.[7]

The Leicestershire VCH chapter was proceeding alongside the work on Lincolnshire, using similar methods, and it appeared in 1954. One of its findings was that enclosure by agreement affected many villages in the county.[8] Joan published articles on Lincolnshire in 1953 about the Isle of Axholme, and in 1955 on Kesteven, culminating in the book *English Peasant Farming*, which dealt with the different regions of the county through successive periods from the sixteenth to the nineteenth century.[9] The research was based on one county, but had a wide significance. It established firmly the importance of regional differences for understanding rural society and agriculture. It showed the value of connecting the various strands of environment, social structure and farming methods to trace long-term changes. It placed country people at the centre of the story; people who could be seen applying intelligence and common sense to their circumstances from an understanding of the land and its qualities.

The next stage was to apply the lessons learnt in Lincolnshire to the whole country. The means by which Hoskins's ambitious plan of 1950 could be implemented came through a project led by his successor, Finberg, who assembled a group of scholars in 1956 to plan and write an *Agrarian History of England and Wales* in many volumes. The senior historians who supported the idea could not find the time to write their contributions, but volume 4, on the period 1500–1640, was assigned to Joan Thirsk as editor.[10] With Lincolnshire complete she had some free time, but more important she was driven by the ideas that had emerged from the Lincolnshire work, in particular the significance of regions, and knew how to obtain results from the local records. By chance, an able cohort of younger historians was available, and they were brought together to achieve a common purpose. In the days before large funded research projects and databases, money

7.   Finberg papers, FIN/6/P/28/5 and /7.
8.   J. Thirsk, 'The agricultural history of Leicestershire', in W.G. Hoskins and R. McKinley (eds), *Victoria history of the county of Leicester*, 2 (London, 1954), pp. 199–264.
9.   J. Thirsk, 'The Isle of Axholme before Vermuyden', *Agricultural History Review*, 1 (1953), pp. 16–28; J. Thirsk, 'Farming in Kesteven, 1540–1640', *Lincolnshire Architectural and Archaeological Society Reports and Papers*, new series, 6 (1955), pp. 37–53; J. Thirsk, *English peasant farming: the agrarian history of Lincolnshire from Tudor to recent times* (London, 1957).
10. J. Thirsk, 'The British Agricultural History Society and *The agrarian history of England and Wales*: new projects in the 1950s', *Agricultural History Review*, 50 (2002), pp. 155–63, especially pp. 159–63.

came from the Nuffield Foundation to employ research assistants, and Margaret Midgley and Alan Everitt travelled to local record offices with a mission to collect data according to a standard template. They reported back to Joan on their progress in the recesses of the British Library, then housed in the British Museum.[11] While she worked on the *Agrarian History* she found time to write a pamphlet on *Tudor Enclosures*, in parallel with her chapter on the same subject for volume 4.[12] By the time she left Leicester in the autumn of 1965 the writing of volume 4 had been completed, although it did not appear until 1967.[13] This, the first volume of the *Agrarian History* to be published, and by far the most influential, was the product of the years Joan spent in Leicester. The idea of an *Agrarian History* had emerged out of Leicester thanks to the persistence and enthusiasm of both Finberg and Thirsk. Finberg served as general editor until his death in 1974 when Joan took on the task, and she saw the whole project, in eight volumes, through to completion in 2000.

When she wrote the chapter on regions for volume 4, Joan was mainly concerned with the farming methods of each part of the country, but she also noticed the local rural industries. She developed a general explanation of the tendency for industry to grow in pastoral landscapes, and contributed an essay on this theme to the festschrift in honour of R.H. Tawney, published in 1961.[14] She argued that animal husbandry demanded less working time than cultivation, and this, together with dense populations encouraged by local inheritance customs, created a work force that could be employed in crafts. She built on this idea in later publications, and the subject was taken up by continental scholars in the 1980s under the banner of 'protoindustrialisation'.

A new venture in her later years at Leicester showed the value of Joan's familiarity with the continental literature. She noted the findings of German historical geographers that field systems in the middle ages developed in an evolutionary fashion under the pressure of population growth and the extension of cultivation. This accorded with her observation of regional variety in farming systems, and cast doubts on the orthodoxy among British historians that the midland field system came ready formed with the Anglo-Saxon migration. She surprised everyone when her article on common fields appeared in 1964, as she was regarded as an early modernist, but more importantly she changed radically the approach to the subject, and set off a new train of thinking that is still influencing us half a century later.[15] The Department of English Local History at

---

11.   A. Everitt, 'Joan Thirsk: a personal appreciation', in J. Chartres and D. Hey (eds), *English rural society: essays in honour of Joan Thirsk* (Cambridge, 1990), pp. 18–20.

12.   J. Thirsk, *Tudor enclosures*, Historical Association pamphlet, general series (London, 1959).

13.   J. Thirsk (ed.), *The agrarian history of England and Wales* (hereafter AHEW), 4: 1500–1640 (Cambridge, 1967).

14.   J. Thirsk, 'Industries in the countryside', in F.J. Fisher (ed.), *Essays in the economic and social history of Tudor and Stuart England in honour of Professor R.H. Tawney* (London, 1961), pp. 70–88.

15.   J. Thirsk, 'The common fields', *Past and Present*, 29 (1964), pp. 3–25.

Leicester was a fertile environment for the development of such new thinking as period divisions were not regarded as barriers, and the notion of locating fields in their social, topographical and demographic context was a commonplace of the 'Leicester approach'. She acknowledged in the footnotes the help given by the ever-supportive Finberg who read drafts and recommended improvements. For her rural industry article she thanked a number of Leicester academics for their advice, including Finberg, Alan Everitt and Norman Scarfe who lectured in the History Department. She was also aided by Rodney Hilton of Birmingham, with whom she had many common interests.

The style and themes of Joan Thirsk's life as a historian can be traced back to her Leicester roots and the work she began as she pursued her main goals at the Lincolnshire project and then with the *Agrarian History* volume. She did not accept orthodoxies and glib general explanations of the past. For generations of historians the main process in early modern agriculture was 'enclosure', by which most historians meant an imposition by a landlord to the detriment of a village. She showed that enclosure took many different forms, and was often (in the seventeenth century) carried out by agreement, but she could still appreciate the resentment and distress that it caused in some parts of the country, especially in the villages of the midlands. She was very conscious of the great movements, such as the rise in population in the sixteenth century, or the growth of towns, but she was anxious to view these events through the eyes of contemporaries, and to appreciate how they regarded their position, and what steps they could take to protect themselves or make changes to gain advantages from new circumstances.[16]

She could see in probate inventories the lists of household possessions, and was conscious that the wealth that farmers acquired from their land was often spent on furnishings, clothing and consumer goods. While working on Lincolnshire she came upon the accounts of a gentry family, the Hatchers of Careby, and observed them buying clothing and spices in London, and obtaining more ordinary goods in towns and at fairs in the region.[17] The industries that were employing so many country people were satisfying demand for a wide range of goods, and especially textiles and clothing. After her time at Leicester, she went on to study consumption and projects designed to satisfy consumer demand.[18]

Her facility in modern languages gave her access to German historians whose writings influenced her thinking about English history, but she also enjoyed literature. When asked why she gave regional differences so much attention, she replied that her reading of German authors showed the importance of regional roots, as writers had a strong sense of the special character of provinces such

16. J. Thirsk, 'My view of economic history', in P. Hudson (ed.), *Living economic and social history* (Glasgow, 2001), pp. 372–5.
17. Thirsk, 'Farming in Kesteven', pp. 51–2.
18. J. Thirsk, *Economic policy and projects: the development of a consumer society in early modern England* (Oxford, 1978).

as Westphalia or Silesia. As well as assembling the reliable but dry data in such sources as inventories, she read contemporary literature and found many helpful comments on farming and the landscape, which added to the attractiveness of her work. For example, her introduction to volume 4 refers to descriptions of the English countryside by continental visitors, who all agreed that they were observing a country populated by fat cows and prosperous peasants.[19]

Joan Thirsk in her Leicester years contributed to the foundation of a number of new institutions, all of which flourished. As well as playing a crucial role in founding the *Agrarian History*, in 1952 she helped to establish together with Finberg the Agricultural History Society, and in 1964 became editor of the *Agricultural History Review*. She became involved in the Deserted Medieval Village Research Group (later the Medieval Settlement Research Group), a valuable bridge between history and archaeology. In 1956 she joined the board of the relatively new journal, *Past and Present*, in which she participated in the selection of articles for publication.[20] She also had an important role in the Standing Conference on Local History, a body that coordinated the activities of many societies and groups of amateur local historians, with whom she had close connections.

The academic profession contained few women in the 1950s, and Joan Thirsk described it as a man's world. She combined remarkably a domestic and a professional life. Her job in Leicester did not require constant attendance, as she was a research fellow. She taught her Special Subject on Tudor Economic and Social History on Wednesdays, and that was her day in Leicester in term time.[21] Throughout her period of employment at Leicester she lived in London, where her husband was employed as a librarian. Their children were born in 1956 and 1958, at the time of the initial work on the *Agrarian History*. The Thirsks employed a 'children's nurse', and her son and daughter remembered a happy upbringing in which their mother was always present. She took no short cuts in household management as she always baked her own bread, and was skilled in needlework – for example, making shirts for her son. Living in London meant that Joan had easy access to the Public Record Office and British Library, and could meet other scholars. On occasion she conferred with Finberg about agrarian history matters, and the business of the Leicester department, as he also lived in London.

Leicester provided Joan Thirsk with a fertile environment for the formation of her ideas and the production of publications, but it was not to last. The Local History Department was a tiny operation connected to the larger History Department with its heavy load of undergraduate teaching. Finberg pointed to the achievements and high academic profile of the Local History Department,

19. Thirsk (ed.), AHEW, 4, pp. xxix–xxxvii.
20. J. Thirsk, 'British Agricultural History Society'; P. Slack, 'Joan Thirsk', *Past and Present*, 222 (2014), pp. 3–7.
21. Information from Professor Roger Richardson who, as an undergraduate, was taught by her.

which did not win him friends among the historians. Finberg was loyal to Joan and lobbied the university to give her increments in her salary, in which he was partly successful. He also sought to have her promoted to a Readership, but those in authority, in particular members of the powerful Establishment Board resisted, apparently because they resented what they saw as her privileged position with few teaching duties. Finberg made some mistakes in his campaign, in particular when he persuaded four very prestigious professors to write on her behalf to the Vice Chancellor.[22] In 1965 a Readership became available at Oxford – ironically the post that Hoskins had held and was now vacating to return to Leicester. Joan's achievements and prospects made her a powerful candidate, and Leicester lost one of its brightest stars.

At Oxford Joan Thirsk engaged a good deal with students, and especially postgraduates, and her research students became a productive and influential presence on the historical scene. In her own research she continued to follow paths that she had opened at Leicester, refining her approach to regions in volume 5 of the *Agrarian History of England and Wales*. At Leicester she had just begun her study of consumers and the industries that fed their demands, and these became major themes in her Oxford days. She developed new subjects such as inheritance and the family, 'projects' and new crops, and horses. After she left Oxford in 1983 she published on a wide range of subjects, among which were major works on 'alternative agriculture' and food. After her Leicester days she became an international academic celebrity, and was deservedly honoured with a fellowship of the British Academy, a CBE and a clutch of honorary doctorates. One of those degrees came from Leicester, where the local historians never forgot their debt to her, and for years after she left they enjoyed the long-term legacy of her 'Agrarian Fellowship'.

22.   Finberg papers FIN/8/2/41/1; FIN/8/Z/41/2, 5, 8, 9, 10, 12, 13, 14.

PART I

Countries, pays and regions: a round table

The editors of this book invited three scholars who had all known Joan Thirsk very well – two of them having been her doctoral students in Oxford – to contribute short papers to a round table on regions. We asked them to consider the historical significance of regions, half a century after she produced her pioneering survey of farming regions in volume 4 of the *Agrarian History* for the period 1500–1640, followed by a more elaborate scheme for the next volume covering the period 1640–1750. We did not give the three historians detailed instructions, but we expected them to show how approaches to the subject had changed, and we hoped that their contributions would reflect a variety of views. They did exactly as we intended, and between them present a range of current thinking about regions.

Hey takes aboard the concept of *pays*, which is the same word as 'country', and which was much used in the early modern period. He emphasises the social and cultural implications of regions, rather than the farming practices and production strategies which were Thirsk's prime concern. He has been a pioneer in the study of family history and especially surnames. He applies the lessons learned from names to answer wider historical questions. In the modern style he applies empathy to early modern people by using their surnames as a way of showing how people were connected to particular districts much smaller than the *pays* and regions studied by Thirsk and her successors. He observes barriers to movement and the limits to people's awareness of a wider world.

Broad pursues the agrarian regions originally investigated by Thirsk, and shows that as useful frames of reference these become less appropriate as we move into the eighteenth and nineteenth centuries. His focus is the counties under the influence of London, and he points out that Thirsk's regions reflected the household-based economies of rural producers, and did not put much emphasis on the influence of towns. He reminds us that, from an early date, urban hinterlands intersected with farming regions, and as towns grew in size they wielded greater influence. He also reminds us that the farming community was stratified – increasingly so after 1700 – and that large- and small-scale farmers had different priorities and varied horizons.

Chartres likewise puts more emphasis than Thirsk on the operations of markets, which became more efficient and influential in the seventeenth and eighteenth centuries. Developments in transport, with better roads and canals, changed the pattern of marketing, and a mature urban hierarchy emerged. The farming regions defined by Thirsk were appropriate to a society with local decision making and relatively restricted horizons. The new commercial world had a longer reach and was organised by middlemen. Towns did much more than generate demand for food and drink for their growing populations, as they entered into the food business with their mills, maltings and breweries, and distributed products so widely that regional differences diminished in significance.

2

Countries and pays

DAVID HEY

One of Joan Thirsk's most influential concepts was that of *pays*, which she developed with Alan Everitt when they were working on volume 4 of *The Agrarian History of England and Wales*. Her maps of agricultural regions showed that the county was not a valid unit for the study of farming practices. Instead, she suggested that historians should point out the contrasts between the various *pays* within a county and they should search for comparisons with districts that had similar soils and settlement patterns beyond the county boundary.

It seems strange that Joan chose a French word for this concept, when the English translation 'country' was in widespread use during the periods that she studied, but of course Joan was a gifted linguist and she was familiar with the work of French agrarian historians. Her postgraduate supervisor, R.H. Tawney used the term, so she may have got it from him. English people had in the twentieth century stopped using 'country' as a term for a neighbourhood with which everyone was familiar, so it was not a natural choice for Joan. The two surviving English examples that are well known do not fit the original concept. The West Country covers far too large an area, and the Black Country was a term of abuse that was invented in the 1840s, probably by someone from Birmingham. Those of us who work on the early modern period have come across the use of the term 'country' time and time again. In his *History of Myddle* Richard Gough used the term naturally in phrases such as 'He was a person well reputed in his country'.[1] The *Oxford English Dictionary* defines this sense of the term as 'A tract or district having more or less definite limits in relation to human occupation, for example owned by the same lord or proprietor, or inhabited by people of the same race, dialect, occupation, etc.' The core groups of families who remained rooted in their 'country' were the ones that shaped local culture and passed on their traditions. They were as important as the nature of the work and of the local landscape in determining the special characteristics of their neighbourhood.

Perhaps we might retain Joan's concept of *pays* when we study agricultural regions, but use 'country' when we are concerned with other matters, such as local

---

1.   R. Gough, *The history of Myddle*, ed. D. Hey (Harmondsworth, 1981), p. 195.

Figure 2.1 Distribution of the surname
Creswick generated from the 1881 census
(n=310)

Figure 2.2 Distribution of the surname
Ackroyd generated from the 1881 census
(n=2802)

speech, traditional building methods and materials, or the concentration of local
industries, as when Daniel Defoe referred to the metalworking district around
Sheffield as 'the country called Hallamshire'?[2]

'Country' is a particularly useful term when studying local demographic
patterns. Population historians have long ago established that people commonly
moved beyond their parish boundaries, but less emphasis is placed on the fact
that most people did not move very far. This is immediately apparent from the
distribution patterns of surnames as late as the 1881 national census, using the
maps provided by Stephen Archer's CD, *The British 19th Century Surname Atlas*.[3]
Two examples from the West Riding of Yorkshire will suffice.

When we look at the national distribution of the Hallamshire surname
Creswick in 1881 (Figure 2.1), we find that it was still concentrated close to its
medieval origin at a farmstead of that name, close to the village of Ecclesfield,
a few miles north of Sheffield. Creswick was the most common surname in the
Elizabethan Sheffield baptism register, and between 1630 and 1667 no fewer than
six Creswicks served as Master Cutler in the Company of Cutlers in Hallamshire.
In the hearth tax returns of 1672, 23 Creswicks were named within Hallamshire,

2.   D. Defoe, *A tour through the whole island of Great Britain* (London, 1962), p. 181.
3.   <http://www.archersoftware.co.uk>.

with one just to the north and four immediately across the Derbyshire border in parishes that are now mostly enclosed within the city of Sheffield. The distribution of the surname remained very tight four centuries or so after Adam de Creswick was first recorded.[4]

By contrast, surnames such as Ackroyd ('oak clearing') are instantly recognisable as names that were derived from medieval farms that were carved out of West Riding woods and moorland edges further north in the textile district (Figure 2.2). In the various Yorkshire hearth tax returns of 1672–3, we find 30 households of Ackroyds, 20 of whom were within walking distance of the home of the name. Others had crossed the Pennines into Lancashire, but 13 Ackroyd households still lived in the ancient parish of Halifax. On the whole, they had not gone far. Ackroyd was an unfamiliar name in the metalworking district of Hallamshire. The name Creswick was unknown in the textile 'country'.

Many more examples could be cited to show that people often moved within their 'country', bounded by the nearest market towns, but that they knew little about life beyond, unless they or other members of their family had been to London. These West Riding families knew nothing about the Yorkshire Dales lead miners or the farmers on the Yorkshire Wolds or in Holderness; indeed, few of them knew anything about the county capital, York. Until the nineteenth century, the concept of the county was familiar to the gentry but not to the masses.

The maps of farming regions that Joan drew for volumes 4 and 5 of the *Agrarian History* show the same type of farming in both the metalworking and the textile parts of the West Riding.[5] They do not differentiate between the Upper Calder valley and Hallamshire. They are accurate enough for their purpose, but the farming *pays* were not the same as the 'countries' that were defined by the major occupations and the core families, nor by speech and some aspects of vernacular architecture. It seems advisable to keep the two terms separate.

As with Joan's agricultural *pays*, the mental world of the 'country' sometimes stretched beyond county boundaries. For example, studies of surname distributions at various points of time, such as the hearth tax returns of 1672, have revealed that the Yorkshire–Lancashire boundary along the Pennine moors was no barrier to movement.[6]

Last year, 'The Peoples of the British Isles' project produced a remarkable map of the various genetic groups that inhabit Britain (Figure 2.3).[7] The authors stressed that the genetic differences between these groups were superficial, yet

4.   D. Hey *et al.* (eds), *West Riding hearth tax assessment, Ladyday 1672*, British Record Society Hearth Tax Series, 5 (2007).
5.   J. Thirsk (ed.), *The agrarian history of England and Wales*, 4: 1500–1640 (Cambridge, 1967) and 5: 1640–1750 (Cambridge, 1985).
6.   G. Redmonds and D. Hey, *Yorkshire surnames and the hearth tax returns of 1672–73* (York, 2002).
7.   <http://www.ox.ac.uk/media/news_stories/2012/120703.html>.

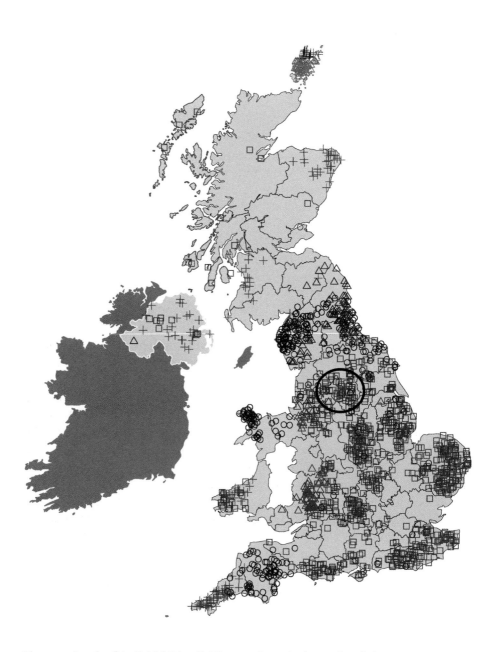

Figure 2.3 People of the British Isles (PoBI) map of genetic clusters in Britain
Note: Reproduced by kind permission of Sir Walter Bodmer.
Sources: W. Bodmer and B. Winney, 'Population genetics: the study of the genetic structure of human populations', eds P. Kreager *et al.*, *Population in the human sciences: concepts, models, evidence* (Oxford, forthcoming), pp. 86–107, at p. 102; S. Leslie *et al.*, 'The fine-scale genetic structure of the British population, *Nature*, 519 (2015), pp. 309–14, at p. 310.

Figure 2.4 Distribution of the surname
Hey generated from the 1881 census
(n=2655)

they were sufficiently pronounced to be observable. A genetic district (marked with an oval) that straddles the Pennines immediately suggests the antiquity of the 'country' that was inhabited by the bearers of such distinctive surnames as Ackroyd, Barraclough and Greenwood, and many others that originated on the Yorkshire side of the moors, and by families such as the Cleggs, the Turtons and the Kershaws, who started from the west. The county boundary was no obstacle to this movement. Is it merely coincidence that the 'country' defined by this genetic group contained these and other families such as the Beardsells, Booths, Buckleys, Butterworths, Chadwicks, Dearnleys, Hamers, Ogdens, Schofields, Sutcliffes, Wardles, Wolstenholmes and Wordsworths, from either side of the county boundary, particularly in the huge parishes of Halifax and Rochdale, where the surnames ramified to a far greater extent than anywhere else in England during the sixteenth and seventeenth centuries?[8]

The boundaries of this generic group are almost identical with the heartland of my own surname in 1881 (Figure 2.4), so it is perhaps no wonder that I am intrigued by this concept of a 'country'. The Heys were West Riding weaver-farmers whose name came from a Pennine moorland farm west of Huddersfield, some 12 miles or so from the parish of Penistone where I lived six centuries later.[9] Having traced all the extended members of my family in the three or four generations after 1800, I discovered that although some of them moved to the textile villages

8.   G. Redmonds, T. King and D. Hey, *Surnames, DNA and family history* (Oxford, 2011), pp. 62–83.
9.   G. Redmonds and D. Hey, 'The opening-up of Scammonden, a Pennine moorland valley', *Landscapes*, 2.1 (2001), pp. 56–73.

nearer Huddersfield and others, particularly the girls, crossed the Pennines to the burgeoning mill town of Glossop, just one of the extended family of Heys moved to the edge of Barnsley, six miles to the east, and only two to the northern suburbs of Sheffield, 10 or 12 miles to the south. The 'country called Hallamshire' was still mostly out of bounds, even though the parish of Penistone stretched as far as its northern boundary. My family story is a fairly typical one from these parts.

3

Joan Thirsk and agricultural regions:
a fifty-year perspective

JOHN BROAD

In 1967 Joan Thirsk published the *Agrarian History of England and Wales* volume 4 covering the period 1500–1640, a work that had an enormous influence on early modern rural history. A striking feature of the volume was her treatment of agricultural regions, and the map of England's farming regions she produced.[1] Joan had mapped farming regions in her first book on Lincolnshire farming in 1957, but it was merely a modified version of the 1944 Land Utilization survey of the area.[2] Mapping historic farming regions on a national scale was a monumental task. John Chartres and I were in Joan's first class in early modern economic history at Oxford in 1965 and were handed out what were probably early drafts of these national maps. Volume 5 of the *Agrarian History*, published in 1984, included a separate regional volume with specialist contributions for different parts of the country. Joan's revised map of farming regions covered Wales as well as England for 1640–1750, while the authors of the regional chapters separately mapped their designated areas.[3] This was the high point of Joan's work on farming regions, but her Economic History Society/Macmillan booklet, aimed at an undergraduate readership, revisited the topic to engage with the more general problems of mapping agrarian regions. In it she engaged with Eric Kerridge's regional map in his *Agricultural Revolution*, provided revised and re-worked maps for the 1500–1640 and 1650–1750 periods, and added a map of farming regions using a 'simplified schedule' based on Alan Everitt's categorisations.[4]

1.   J. Thirsk (ed.), *The agrarian history of England and Wales* (hereafter AHEW), 4: 1500–1640 (Cambridge, 1967), p. 4.
2.   J. Thirsk, *English peasant farming: the agrarian history of Lincolnshire from Tudor to recent times* (London, 1957), p. 50.
3.   J. Thirsk (ed.), AHEW, 5: 1640–1750, 2 parts (Cambridge, 1984), pp. xx–xxi.
4.   J. Thirsk, *Agricultural regions and agrarian history in England, 1500–1750* (Basingstoke, 1987); E. Kerridge, *The agricultural revolution* (London, 1967); A.M. Everitt, 'Reflections on the historical origin of regions and pays', *Journal of Historical Geography*, 3/1 (1977), pp. 1–19.

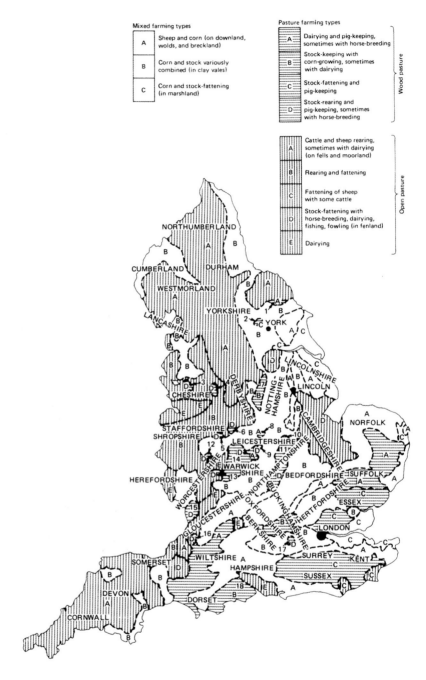

Figure 3.1(a) Joan Thirsk's updated (1987) farming regions 1500–1640
Source: Thirsk, *Agricultural regions*, pp. 28 and 31.

Figure 3.1(b) Joan Thirsk's updated (1987) farming regions 1640–1750
Source: Thirsk, *Agricultural regions*, pp. 28 and 31.

Joan's maps of farming regions were central to her approach to the agrarian history of England and Wales. Putting her achievements into context almost fifty years on enriches our perspective. Joan Thirsk began her historical career under R.H. Tawney at the London School of Economics (LSE) and continued at the newly formed Department of English Local History at Leicester, under the influence of H.P.R. Finberg and W.G. Hoskins. It could be said that in the fifties and sixties the two departments diverged in their approach to early modern English economic history. At the LSE the departure of Tawney led to Jack Fisher becoming head of department. A man of very considerable scholarship, his important work emphasised London as the fulcrum for economic activity and growth in the early modern English economy.[5] He once said that he could not complete his great project of writing a history of London without writing a history of England. Hoskins, on the other hand, had a deep hostility towards things metropolitan, and, although as a fine economic and social historian he never ignored London, he put regions and localities at the centre of his approach. His contributions to the VCH, and his essays and books on English local history reflected this. While Joan continued to be London-based when she worked in Leicester, the influence of the Leicester school was apparent in her work on Lincolnshire, and her bottom-up approach went hand-in-hand with a life-long dedication to the practice of local history and cooperation with local historians.

Joan's monumental mapping of English farming regions brought together the two approaches. Part of her differentiation of regional farming reflected the importance of markets and fairs as their focus shifted from a service for the local area (or 'pays') to a conduit that fed London and other towns, as Defoe's account of early eighteenth-century England compellingly illustrated.[6] Yet London, Lincoln and York are the only urban centres marked on volume 4's regional map and no towns are displayed in volume 5 (Figures 3.1(a) and (b)).

Other useful comparisons can be made between the map produced in volume 4 and that in volume 5. The basic regions remain identifiable in both, but volume 5 makes finer distinctions with additional areas. The map in volume 5 added a new element to the classification of regions, 'subsistence' farming in some otherwise market-oriented agrarian systems, but it is unclear how far differences between the two maps reflect changes in agrarian structure and specialisation between 1600 and 1700, or indicate Joan's more detailed appreciation of local agrarian difference almost twenty years on. Joan recognised the difficulties. In her introduction to the regional section of volume 5, she wrote 'it is not easy to differentiate farming specialities with great accuracy, especially since the systems of large and small farmers in the same region could vary considerably'. More

5.   F. J. Fisher, *London and the English economy, 1500–1700*, eds P.J. Corfield and N.B. Harte (London, 1990).

6.   D. Defoe, *A tour through the whole island of Great Britain*, ed. P. Rodgers (Harmondsworth, 1978).

ruefully, she reflected that her specialist regional chapters had not sustained her national overview: 'authors on either side of a county frontier have not always agreed in their identification of the dominant local farming type'.[7]

Joan always described her regions as 'very tentative'. How far did her farming regions reflect rural historians' hindsight on a vanished world, rather than how it was understood by contemporaries? The word *'pays'* used by the Leicester Local History school, a curious French coinage to delineate a very English concept, has been used in ways cultural, linguistic and social as well as economic. They demarcated a world of small market towns and their hinterlands, the essence of Hoskins' *Provincial England*, with deliberately fluid boundaries reflecting a number of factors. Farmers chose their markets according to their specialisms, not geographical proximity, and Alan Everitt and John Chartres' studies of agricultural marketing demonstrated how market areas overlapped because markets had specialised.[8]

In what period contemporaries began to recognise farming regions precisely is not easy to answer. Robert Plot's late seventeenth-century county histories of Oxfordshire and Staffordshire differentiate different geologies and countrysides, but less obviously farming regions.[9] Defoe's renowned early eighteenth-century *Tour* draws attention to the varied agriculture of England, but usually in the context of their trade with London. The first explicit differentiation may be William Ellis's *Chiltern and Vale Farming Explained*, which contrasted the farming methods of the two halves of Buckinghamshire in 1733.[10] Later in the century the career of the plebian farming clergyman, John Mastin, demonstrates how geographical mobility fostered appreciation of regional farming difference. He grew up on a farm between Nottingham and Newark, but later lived in Countesthorpe, south of Leicester.[11] In his mid-twenties, Mastin managed an estate near Rickmansworth in Hertfordshire, but on marriage returned to his father's adopted Leicestershire village where he built a house on a smallholding. On ordination he found a curacy in Market Bosworth, and later became rector of Naseby across the Northamptonshire border. When he went to Hertfordshire:

> the mode of agriculture, and implements of husbandry were equally strange.
> The two-wheeled plows of the county were almost prodigies, and the knee-

7. Thirsk (ed.), AHEW, 5, part 1, p. xxi.
8. W.G. Hoskins, *Provincial England: essays in social and economic history* (Basingstoke, 1965); Thirsk (ed.), AHEW, 4, chapter 8; Thirsk (ed.), AHEW, 5, part 2, pp. 406–502.
9. R. Plot, *The natural history of Oxfordshire* (Oxford, 1676); R. Plot, *The natural history of Staffordshire* (Oxford, 1686).
10. W. Ellis, *Chiltern and vale farming explained* (London, 1733).
11. J. Mastin, *A Georgian country parson: the Rev. John Mastin of Naseby*, ed. C. Vialls and K. Collins; with a note on the Battle of Naseby by Glenn Foard (Northampton, 2004), pp. 6–14. His father was evicted from the Nottinghamshire farm.

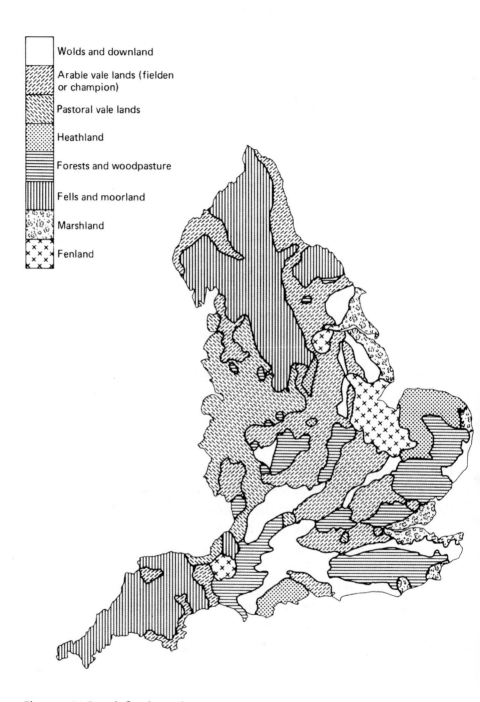

Figure 3.2(a) Generic farming regions
Source: Thirsk, *Agricultural regions*, p. 39.

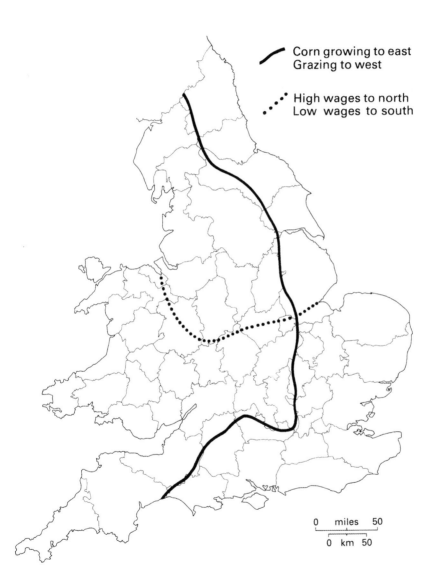

Corn growing to east
Grazing to west

High wages to north
Low wages to south

0   miles   50

0   km   50

Figure 3.2(b) Caird's farming divisions, 1851

Source: J. Caird, English agriculture in 1850–1 (London,1851), frontispiece.

fan he had never before seen. The method of cleansing corn by throwing, he was quite unaccustomed to; and many of their terms he did not understand.[12]

Later, as well as performing his clerical duties, he acted as a land agent and 'man of country business'. In 1794 he advised a Mr Sturges who:

> had imbibed a rage, amounting almost to a mania, for farming, and had a very favourable idea of commencing business in Hertfordshire; a Hertfordshire Farmer was in his opinion a most respectable character; far surpassing in morality and manners the purse-proud Graziers of his own country.[13]

Perversely, Mastin, who had specialised in improving newly enclosed arable grounds in several locations, decided to change his own mode of farming in the same year, selling his wife's land to raise capital to set up a new 'business of grasier' which he continued for the next thirty years. Mastin was certainly aware of the different regional patterns of farming, but equally that in any given farming '*pays*' there were farmers operating quite different business models and specialisations.

Under Joan's general editorship, volumes 6 and 7 of the *Agrarian History* provided no national map of agricultural specialisation and concentrated on the contemporary discovery of regional difference, perhaps because the wider diffusion of new agricultural techniques, by press, books, journeys and personal contact, reduced local variation in favour of 'High Farming' systems.[14] Caird's classic delineation of farming types in 1851 was much simpler, dividing the country into four quarters to reflect two simple factors: a wet pastoral west and dry arable east, and a high wage north and a low wage south (Figures 3.2(a) and (b)).

Joan Thirsk's maps of agricultural regions were path-breaking and have remained highly influential. Her regions were never definitive, but guidelines to an approach and subject to revision. They seem to reflect the Hoskins tradition that tended to minimise, without ignoring, London's vast influence on agricultural change. Interestingly, although she was a fluent German speaker and often reviewed books on German rural history, Joan's agricultural regions never reflected Von Thunen's ideas on how cities influence the adjacent types of agriculture though an English translation was available in 1966.[15] Was this because her agricultural regions primarily reflected a view that the majority of farmers were first and foremost providing for their families, and were not the rising tenant farmers focused on the market? This would chime well with her view

---

12. Mastin, *Georgian country parson*, p. 15.
13. Mastin, *Georgian country parson*, p. 39.
14. e.g. Hugh Prince in G.E. Mingay (ed.), *AHEW*, 6: 1750–1850 (Cambridge, 1989), chapter 1.
15. J.H. von Thünen, C.M. Wartenberg and P. Hall, *Von Thunen's 'Isolated State': an English edition of Der Isolierte Staat* (Oxford, 1966).

that alternative agriculture was driven by small farmers.[16] She knew that within her farming regions some larger farmers practised a specialised agriculture very different from the majority. By the eighteenth century, the farming systems of parishes that had converted to pasture after enclosure differed from their open-field neighbours and her maps probably underplay the importance of, for instance, dairying.[17] There may also be differences in the regions Joan marked as similar because of climate and diet. For instance, the arable regions of the north, particularly the north-west, were primarily oat-growing rather than wheat and barley producers (Figures 3.3(a) and (b) *see over page*). It is not something that her maps were designed to show.

As we follow in Joan's footsteps, probing the relationship between the local traditions of farming, the impact of new crops and livestock, new land management techniques and above all the rising influence of the market as London and the new industrial towns grew, we perhaps need a new paradigm that layers the types of enterprise in any given area: those on smallholdings, those in enclosed areas rather than the open fields and those of the larger, more market-oriented farmers. New techniques of computer mapping and GIS may help facilitate an alternative approach by allowing multiple representations of farming systems in the same area.

16. J. Thirsk, *Alternative agriculture: a history from the Black Death to the present day* (Oxford, 1997).
17. J. Broad, 'Regional perspectives and variations in English dairying, 1650–1850', in R.W. Hoyle (ed.), *People, landscape and alternative agriculture: essays for Joan Thirsk* (Exeter, 2004), pp. 93–112.

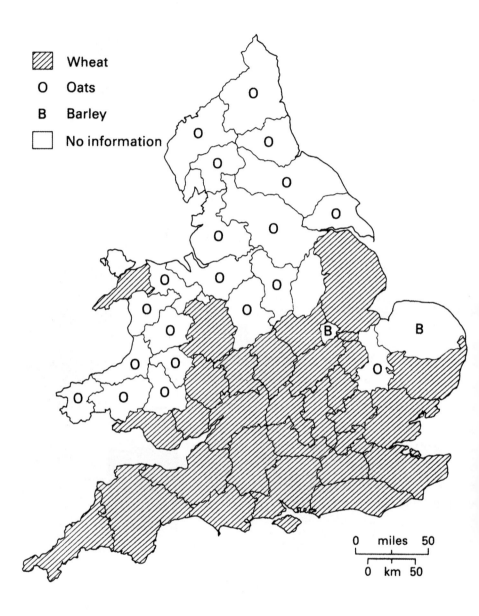

Figure 3.3(a) Main arable crops in different parts of England and Wales
Source: AHEW, 6, 1750–1850 (Cambridge, 1989), p. 39, Fig, 1.13.

Figure 3.3(b) English dairying regions, c.1800

Source: Reworked by the author from Broad, 'Regional perspectives', pp. 102–7.

4

Joan Thirsk: pays, country, transitions and agencies

JOHN CHARTRES

In 1967, Joan Thirsk published her survey and definition of 'The farming regions of England' in the first volume of the *Agrarian History* to be published. This included a map describing the typology of land use, defining the regions by reference to three types of mixed farming, four 'wood pasture' groups of livestock farming, and five separate groups of open pasture, all presented as summaries of the broad characteristics for the period as a whole, within the discussion of which critical elements of change were identified. The survey was significant in looking at farming types without direct reference to the counties that had formed the basis for most previous studies.[1] Farming 'regions' thus included different types of *pays*, more directly relevant to practical agriculture and life, and defined by social and economic processes, not the political structures of county government. Both John Broad and I had the delight of encountering these findings, modified for the end of the seventeenth century, in the maps Joan handed out in her 1965 Oxford undergraduate class on Defoe and his *Tour*, drawn by hand with Chinagraph pencil onto Ordnance Survey quarter-inch bases.

This approach was developed in volume 5 of the *Agrarian History* published in 1984 with the analysis of 'farming regions', 1640–1750, but using a different taxonomy: pastoral, intermediate and arable, producing in all 18 types in a much more detailed map, supported by 11 specialist chapters on England and one, as in volume 4, on Wales, this time subdivided by groups of county.[2] This established regions as a continuing element of the *Agrarian Histories*, with Hugh Prince's chapter in volume 6, 1750–1850, comparing a mid-eighteenth-century base with Caird's contemporary analysis of the 1850s, and the Royal Agricultural Society

---

1. J. Thirsk (ed.), *The agrarian history of England and Wales* (hereafter AHEW), 4: 1500–1640 (Cambridge, 1967), pp. 1–15.
2. J. Thirsk (ed.), AHEW, 5: 1640–1750 (Cambridge, 1984), part I.

prize essays with regions of larger size defined by economy and soils.[3] Other approaches appeared in the work of Eric Kerridge, which identified differing farming 'countries', and Mark Overton's 1996 survey, which added Thirsk's map of *pays* (1987), a simplified representation of the 'regions' of volume 5.[4] The net effect of these studies was to provide a series of cross-sections descriptive of basic farming types and practices across more than three centuries of change.

These studies represented a changing series of districts of the kind first defined by Alfred Marshall, each with its own distinctive economy and internal efficiency. Although applied to the classic industrial district, Anna Markusen's reworking of 'industrial districts', never fully articulated by Marshall himself, works well as a descriptor of the internal coherence of agrarian regions at their successive stages of development.[5] It described the principal elements of our farming regions: small and locally owned or controlled enterprises, with modest economies to scale and substantial intra-district trade; local investment decision-making; long-term commitment and contracting between buyers and sellers, with a comparatively low degree of external linkages; a highly flexible local labour market in which workers were committed to districts not firms; strong local cultural identity; specialised services, finance and technical expertise, with relatively 'patient' capital available within the locality. Such a description of agrarian regions fitted well with the series derived from Joan Thirsk's work and that of the other authors of the *Agrarian Histories*, and here can form the template for discussions of change over time, from the later fifteenth to the mid-nineteenth century.

Each volume of the series also contained a chapter on marketing, each different in approach, but identifying one of the key dynamic elements in the system of regional change and rural innovation. During the period considered here, six such changes influenced agrarian society, some more obviously linked to the Thirsk legacy than others. Within farming society there was a shift towards commercial livestock farming from the fifteenth century, when, as Dyer suggested, rising disposable incomes created rising demand for protein and fats in the English diet.[6] Middlemen and commercial agents grew in number and, from the middle

3. G.E. Mingay (ed.), AHEW, 6: 1750–1850, chapter 1, 'The changing rural landscape, 1750–1850', pp. 7–83.

4. E. Kerridge, *The agricultural revolution* (London, 1967), frontispiece and pp. 41–180; M. Overton, *Agricultural revolution in England: the transformation of the agrarian economy 1500–1800* (Cambridge, 1996), pp. 10–62.

5. A. Markusen, 'Sticky places in slippery space: a typology of industrial districts', *Economic Geography*, 72 (1996), pp. 293–313; A. Marshall, *Principles of economics*, 1 (London, 1890) and *Industry and trade: a study of industrial technique and business organization, and of their influences on the conditions of various classes and nations* (London, 1919).

6. C. Dyer, *Making a living in the middle ages: the people of Britain 850–1520* (New Haven and London, 2002).

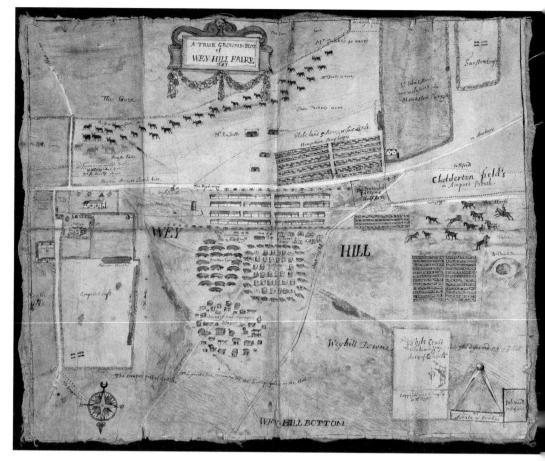

Figure 4.1 'A True Ground Plot of Wey Hill Faire', 1683
Source: Reproduced by permission of Queen's College Library and Archives, Oxford.

years of the seventeenth century, operational freedom to enhance the effectiveness of food markets, with, as Thwaites has suggested, a continuation of the practice of licensing with greater operational freedom.[7] The period experienced growing and changing local and regional specialisation, especially during England's emergence as the most rapidly urbanising country of Europe after 1600, and, by the end of the eighteenth century, the emergence of a mature urban hierarchy, in which the relative size of England's towns conformed to log-linearity, a clear indicator of spatial efficiency.[8]

7.   W. Thwaites, 'Dearth and the marketing of agricultural produce: Oxfordshire *c.* 1750–1800', *Agricultural History Review*, 33 (1985), pp. 119–31.
8.   J. de Vries, *European urbanization 1500–1800* (London, 1984), *passim.*

These issues can be identified in contemporary observations of regional and interregional trade, as illustrated here by Figure 4.1, 'A True Ground Plot of Wey Hill Faire' of 1683. Within this map, one can observe exactly these commercial developments. Situated on the Ridgeway south of Winchester between Andover and Amesbury, this was a fair that reflected these changes, and a commercial institution that survived into the 1920s. In the centre, north of the Ridgeway, lay the 'Hampshire Sheep Coopes', with Dorset sheep to the south-east and the horse fair north of them, and a separate set of pens for North Wiltshire sheep next to a long range of commercial buildings for goods, trades and entertainment. Separate zones in the fairground can be observed for manufactures, hops, leather and leather goods, cheese, and joinery and turners' wares. It described a fairground similar to the near-contemporary survey of Sturbridge Fair, on the outskirts of Cambridge (dated 1725).[9]

These maps of fairs at the top of the commercial hierarchy indicated extensive supply zones and commercial agency. Similar patterns were emerging in the mercantile groups of the market towns, in which weekly rather than seasonal transactions took place, increasingly in the private markets of emergent wholesale trades in the long eighteenth century. After the middle of the seventeenth century, these towns enjoyed enhanced commercial centrality as a result of large-scale river 'navigation', new road systems in the turnpikes, improved ports on the coast and, from the 1750s, the development of canals to further improve inland navigation and turn England 'outside in' by providing transport systems highly suited to cereal traffic akin to that which had pre-existed in the coastwise trade. These extensive transport changes aided the differentiation of urban functions, and helped some towns to become more influential in agriculture than others. Ahead of many English towns that became the central servicing locations of the emerging industrial zones, these towns served farming in similar ways.

If, for the sake of argument, it is accepted that the urban system shifted from the concave distribution, characterised by the London-dominated sixteenth century, towards the remarkably even linearity of the second quarter of the nineteenth century, then some agriculture-servicing towns stood out from this general pattern. General patterns of spatial efficiency that emerged in this period still left some locations more dominant in agricultural trades than others, and led to clusterings of middlemen and processing businesses within them. The example of the West Riding of Yorkshire, where there were also many emergent industrial centres, thoroughfare towns, and inland ports sustains the point.[10] A significant subset of these Yorkshire towns stood out by 1821 as the locations of cereal processing and traffic. Rotherham had one cereal-processing business in

9.   Map of Sturbridge Fair, 1725, Oxford, Bodleian Library, Gough Maps 2 fol.10.
10. E. Baines, Baines's Yorkshire: a new printing of the two volumes of history, directory and gazetteer of the county of York (Leeds, 1822, reproduced Newton Abbot and East Ardsley, Wakefield, 1969), I, West Riding.

1821 for every 141 of its population; Pontefract, 171; Wakefield, 182; Ripon, 304; Knaresborough, 310; Doncaster, 329; Thorne, 385; and Tadcaster, at this date yet to emerge as a major brewing centre, 404. Specialisation in the urban centres of major corn-growing regions thus acted as a distinctive force for wider changes in parallel with the emergence of wider changes in urban function.

These towns that were providing specialised marketing services to 'improving' agricultural regions often lay in the middle ranks of the new urban patterns of the second quarter of the nineteenth century, but the larger urban centres also continued to have a role. Leeds, the increasingly dominant urban centre of the West Riding – in textiles, other industry, business services and so on – retained large and increasingly larger-scale grain processors. In 1821, within a much more diverse economy than the processing centres described above, Leeds had a cereal-processing business for every 828 of its inhabitants, adding up to 79 separate firms. The smaller, but still more industrially focused town of Sheffield, averaged food processors at half the Leeds rate, one to every 1,865 inhabitants, but it still had 35, and this cluster appeared greater still if the contiguous dealers and processors of Rotherham were added to it. These centres exemplified the agencies of rural specialisation and change described by Joan Thirsk's 'regions' and pointed to the clustering of trading services that permitted the shifting and intensifying land use that allowed England to remain largely self-sufficient in food before 1850.

This survey has argued that it is important further to integrate the agency of dealing and transport services into Joan Thirsk's picture of regional systems, and for those discussed by Hugh Prince for the period up to 1850. The second quarter of the nineteenth century experienced the decline of both the protoindustrial economy and the highly successful era of agricultural improvement. From the 1820s, there were the beginnings of steam-milling and similar forms of large-scale processing. By mid-century, there existed an integrated set of 'industrial' malting, based upon the Trent and Ouse river systems and the east coast grain trades.[11] Thereafter, as Britain increasingly came to source its bread grains from abroad, trade in agricultural goods once more turned 'inside out', with milling and processing shifting to the importing ports from which rail distribution moved foodstuffs to the inland towns, and, as Caird demonstrated, England's farming regions changed once more into a smaller number of much larger regions. The era of Joan Thirsk's 'farming countries' came to an end after 1850.

11. Mingay (ed.), *AHEW*, 6, pp. 397–415 and 501–19; E.J.T. Collins (ed.), *AHEW*, 7, part 2 (Cambridge, 2000), pp. 1060–100; C. Clark, *The British malting industry since 1830* (London, 1998).

PART II

Farmers and fields

5

Joan Thirsk and 'The common fields'

TOM WILLIAMSON

Few academic articles can have been as influential as 'The common fields', which Joan Thirsk published in the journal *Past and Present* in 1964.[1] It represented a fundamental shift in approach to the study of medieval field systems, and it continues to be a major influence on our thinking. Some aspects of the article's argument, it is true, were challenged over the succeeding decades, but more recent research has often served to confirm Thirsk's original views. On other matters she does now appear, in hindsight, to have been mistaken, but even here perhaps because she failed to follow through the logic of her own model. More than half a century on, 'The Common Fields' continues to be read, discussed and referenced in the principal literature on medieval agriculture, and continues to inspire fresh insights.

Open fields, which may be defined as areas of arable land containing intermixed properties in the form of narrow unenclosed strips, subject to rights of common grazing and other communal controls, were widespread if not ubiquitous in medieval and early post-medieval England, and took a wide variety of forms. Their character and origins had already been studied by historians for many decades before Thirsk's seminal article appeared. Most attention had focused on the most rigorously organised variety, which was found in the central areas of England, in a band of territory extending from the north-east of the country, through the Midlands, down to the south coast. In this version, the fields were extensive and continuous, accounting for most or all of the arable land in a township. The narrow strips – selions or 'lands' – were grouped into blocks called furlongs or shotts, which were in turn aggregated into larger units called 'fields', usually two or three in number, one of which lay fallow each year and was grazed in common by the livestock of the community. In the middle ages, each farm comprised a large number of strips scattered evenly, and sometimes very regularly, across the area of the township. Strong communal controls were exercised over farming routines, including the exploitation of the common 'waste' lying beyond the fields. Such an agricultural system, so alien to modern concepts of ownership and land management, understandably attracted historical attention

1.   J. Thirsk, 'The common fields', *Past and Present*, 29 (1964), pp. 3–29.

from an early date. But, as Thirsk and others were well aware by the 1960s, other forms of open-field farming were practised to either side of the Midland belt, which were first categorised and discussed by Howard Gray in 1915.[2] In these, holdings were less evenly scattered across the township, the open arable was often accompanied by or interspersed with enclosed parcels of land, and communal controls were often, although not always, less rigorous and pervasive in character. Perhaps not surprisingly, these divergences from Midland practice were associated with significant differences in the character of settlement, which were noted but seldom emphasised by early scholars. The extensive and highly communal field systems of the Midland regions were generally farmed from nucleated villages; the various alternatives were associated with more dispersed forms of settlement, featuring small hamlets and outlying farms in addition to, and sometimes instead of, villages.

Up until the publication of 'The common fields', there was consensus that the various forms of medieval field system had very early, pre-Conquest origins. Seebohm in the 1880s believed that open-field agriculture developed in the Roman period, through the need of peasant cultivators to share plough teams and ploughs.[3] Vinogradoff in contrast argued that the intermixture of properties arose from a primitive concept of tribal shareholding.[4] Both these writers concentrated their attention on the well-developed fields of the Midlands; it was Gray who expanded his interests to embrace the other types of field system. The different agrarian arrangements revealed in medieval documents represented, he believed, the areas settled by particular tribal groups in the post-Roman period. The 'Midland System' – Gray's term for the classic, village-based open fields found in the central districts of the country – had thus been imported fully formed from the Anglo-Saxon homelands in northern Germany and southern Scandinavia, and its concentration in these central districts reflected their 'thorough Germanisation' in the fifth and sixth centuries.[5] The irregular, patchwork systems found in places like Kent and East Anglia, in contrast, represented existing Romano-British patterns of land holding, in which properties had subsequently fragmented through the effects of partible inheritance, although in East Anglia a subsequent wave of Danish settlement, resulting in a high density of free tenures and complex manorial arrangements, had led to further changes.[6] Not all explanations advanced in the first half of the twentieth century, however, placed quite such an emphasis on nebulous 'cultural' concepts. In particular, the Orwins, whose book *The Open Fields* appeared in 1938, argued like Seebohm that communal field systems

---

2. H.L. Gray, *English field systems* (Cambridge, MA, 1915).
3. F. Seebohm, *The English village community* (London, 1883), pp. 120–2 and 409–11.
4. P. Vinogradoff, *Villeinage in England* (Oxford, 1892), p. 236; P. Vinogradoff, *The growth of the manor* (London, 1905), p. 150.
5. Gray, *English field systems*, p. 415.
6. Gray, *English field systems*, pp. 415–17.

arose from the need to share ploughs, although they believed that this had only become important during the post-Roman period, when the heavy mouldboard plough came into widespread use. They noted – as others had done – the intimate connection between the division of land *as strips* and the use of a large wheeled plough, difficult to manoeuvre in small enclosed parcels.[7] They also argued, more generally, that villages and open fields reflected the need for cooperation by pioneer farmers in a hostile environment; and they thus placed the origins of Gray's 'Midland System' well before the Norman Conquest.

At the time 'The common fields' was published there was thus general agreement that medieval field systems had early, pre-Conquest origins. Many historians, moreover, also accepted the importance of race and tribal custom in the genesis of regional variations in their character. Thirsk's article challenged such assumptions, for she argued that open fields, at least in their fully developed form, only emerged some time *after* the Norman Conquest. And rather than having been created, or imported, fully formed, the most complex field systems of medieval England had developed gradually over time.

Thirsk's model

Thirsk began by distinguishing various forms of open-field agriculture, effectively re-casting Gray's classification but in a functional rather than explicitly geographical or 'racial' way. She distinguished what she called 'common fields' from other kinds of field system, identifying their four key elements: the existence of arable land, and meadow land, divided into strips held by different tenants; the practice of common pasturing on both, after the crops had been harvested or the hay cut; the common use of the 'wastes' or common lands beyond the arable; and the administration of the whole complex system by a manorial court or village assembly.[8] Other aspects were implied in such a definition, or followed from these features, most notably enforced rotations across extensive and continuous areas, so that they could be grazed in common not only immediately after harvest, but also during a fallow season. In large measure the system she defined was that found in the central districts of England, Gray's 'Midland System', although not entirely, for her definition could in theory embrace townships with multiple field systems, operated from a number of hamlets. In practice, however, what she discussed was the more complex and communal forms of open field, the two- or three-field systems associated with large villages.

Having noted the presence of a variety of agricultural systems in medieval England, and describing the characteristics of true 'common fields', Thirsk proceeded to question the kinds of early origins suggested by Gray or Seebohm and implied by the Orwins. In particular, she argued that while some elements of

7.   C.S. Orwin and C.S. Orwin, *The open fields* (Oxford, 1938).
8.   Thirsk, 'Common fields', pp. 3–4.

the common-field system may have originated at a very early date, they had only been combined into a fully functioning whole in the post-Conquest period. In part this belief was based on a particular aspect of Thirsk's scholarship which deserves to be noted: her interest in and knowledge of European research, something that arose directly from her earlier studies of modern languages. She thus cited recent German works, both archaeological and historical, which suggested that in the Iron Age settlement in that country had mainly taken the form of single farms or small hamlets, and that these had only developed into villages during the early middle ages, as a consequence of population growth. Demographic expansion had also led to the formation of farms which, rather than comprising single plots of land, adopted the pattern of small intermingled parcels. There were two reasons for this. First, the expansion in the area under cultivation, which was needed to feed a growing population, led to the reclamation or 'assarting' of areas of woodland and waste which – because they had formerly been grazed and otherwise exploited in common, and because their clearance and conversion to ploughland had been a joint endeavour – were shared between groups of cultivators in the form of strips. Secondly, and perhaps more importantly, as the population grew farms were divided by partible inheritance – they were shared between all sons – in an equitable manner, allocating to each a reasonable share of near and distant land, and land of variable aspect and quality. This process, repeated over several generations, likewise led (given the character of the large plough now in widespread use) to the emergence of areas of intermingled strips. In both cases, strips were unhedged because of their small size, and because fences or hedges would have limited the manoeuvrability of the plough, taken up a significant amount of land, and – given the number of strips held by an individual, and the total length of fencing or hedging needed – would have presented insuperable problems of maintenance. Further intermixture of properties had resulted from the frequent buying, selling and exchange of property which had characterised early peasant society.[9]

Once the land of a community had developed as a complex intermixture of properties, the need for some measure of cooperation and agreement over grazing and crop rotations soon followed, initially between neighbours, and then more generally. Such a need would have become particularly pressing as arable continued to expand at the expense of common pastures, for this would have placed increasing importance on the grazing provided by harvest residues and arable weeds. It would have been hard for one farmer to introduce livestock onto his lands after harvest if the strips of his neighbours were still occupied by standing crops; impossible to graze a strip lying fallow, if adjacent lands were under cultivation. Thirsk wrote:

9.   Thirsk, 'Common fields', pp. 8–9.

Eventually, as fields multiplied whenever new land was taken into cultivation from the waste, and as the parcels of each cultivator became more and more scattered, regulations had to be introduced to ensure that all had access to their own land and to water, and that meadows and ploughland were protected from damage by stock. The community was drawn together by sheer necessity to cooperate in the control of farming practices. All the fields were brought together into two or three large units. A regular crop rotation was agreed by all and it became possible to organise more efficiently the grazing of stubble and aftermath. Thereafter, the scattering of strips, which had at one time been a handicap, became a highly desirable arrangement, since it gave each individual a proportion of land under each crop in the rotation.[10]

Thirsk argued, in essence, that a similar pattern of development had occurred in England. She provided evidence for the early appearance of arable land divided into strips, and proposed that in England, as in Germany, this largely arose from the practice of partible inheritance.[11] Intermixed areas of arable and meadow land, probably although not certainly in the form of strips, existed by the late seventh century, to judge from the wording of a law issued by King Ine of Wessex, which describes how some ceorls held 'common meadow or other land divided into shares', and shared between them the responsibility for maintaining the stock-proof fence which surrounded the areas in question.[12] But it was only towards the end of the Saxon period that charters suggest the development of very extensive areas of intermixed arable. In a situation in which detailed evidence was in short supply, Thirsk employed a rigorous, forensic logic. If her model was broadly correct, then fully developed common fields could only have developed later rather than earlier in the medieval period, because their emergence was a consequence of population growth and pressure on resources, and she quoted Finberg's suggestion that the area under cultivation at Hawling in Gloucestershire grew by six times between the eleventh century and the time that the earliest map was surveyed in the eighteenth century. She suggested that various documents from the twelfth and thirteenth centuries revealed 'some of the steps in the development of a common-field system', and concluded that 'we can point to the twelfth and first half of the thirteenth century as possibly the crucial ones in the development of the first common-field systems'.[13] In other words, far from having origins in the early Anglo-Saxon period, the highly complex open fields, which, in particular, characterised the Midland districts of England, had only developed in the post-Conquest period and were, to a large extent, a product of the great surge in population of the high middle ages.[14]

10. Thirsk, 'Common fields', p. 14.
11. Thirsk, 'Common fields', pp. 12–15.
12. Whitelock, *English historical documents*, 1, 500–1042 (London, 1955), p. 368.
13. Thirsk, 'Common fields', p. 23.
14. Thirsk, 'Common fields', p. 24.

The adoption of a two- or three-field system in which a half, or a third, of the arable lands lay fallow each year as a continuous block, would have necessitated some reorganisation of land holding, so that the strips of each cultivator were scattered fairly evenly through the arable. This was because if a farmer's lands were mainly concentrated in one section of the arable (as might well have been the case where original holdings had splintered under the impact of partible inheritance) then the imposition of a large, continuous fallowing sector would have ensured that every second or third year most or all of his lands lay uncultivated. Thirsk suggested that this redistribution of properties might have been achieved piecemeal, over a period of time, through sale and exchange. But she also acknowledged that the documentary evidence indicated that in some cases it resulted from wholesale, planned reorganisation: late medieval documents revealed that in many Midland field systems the holdings followed a regular sequence, repeated across the furlongs, which could only have been a consequence of conscious design.[15] Yet even such signs of regular layout were not necessarily evidence for lordly planning. As she noted:

> there is no reason to think that the social framework in which common-field systems emerged necessarily influenced their form. They could evolve in a highly authoritarian society, in which the lord allotted land to his men ... They could just as well take shape in a society of free colonists.[16]

The reception

Thirsk's elegant model was immediately influential. Indeed, the rapidity with which it was accepted by scholars working in both history and historical geography is clear from a cursory perusal of Baker and Butlin's *Studies in British Field Systems*, published in 1973.[17] All of the contributors to this volume seemed to concur with Thirsk's model, at least to some extent. But within a few years of this book's publication some researchers, while not necessarily questioning the basics of Thirsk's model, were querying some of its details, and suggesting amendments. In the 1981 volume edited by Trevor Rowley, *The Origins of Open-field Agriculture*, Bruce Campbell questioned the extent to which the redistribution of strips, to allow the imposition of a continuous fallowing sector, could have been the consequence of gradual, piecemeal development, and instead saw the hand of lordship as a key factor in the shaping of this and other kinds of medieval field system. In the same volume, Harold Fox – in a magisterial analysis of the documentary evidence, especially early charters – raised questions about Thirsk's chronology for open-field genesis:

15. Thirsk, 'Common fields', pp. 20–1.
16. Thirsk, 'Common fields', p. 24.
17. A.R.H. Baker and R.A. Butlin (eds), *Studies of field systems in the British Isles* (Cambridge, 1973).

By the tenth century, more complicated systems with intermixed acre strips had developed in some townships, and it is possible that at some of these places a two- or three-field system had been or was about to be put in place. At the end of the twelfth century there can be no doubt that the system was fully developed both in its organisation and its extent.[18]

By this time, moreover, archaeologists working in the Midland county of Northamptonshire – Glenn Foard and David Hall – were suggesting an even earlier chronology. Systematic fieldwalking revealed that the initial Anglo-Saxon settlement pattern in the area had not consisted of nucleated villages with houses in tight clusters. Instead, numerous small sites were represented by pottery scatters located away from the modern settlements – single farms or small hamlets which had later been over-ploughed as a result of the medieval open-field system.[19] Nucleated villages had evidently come into existence at some later period, although – given the difficulties of dating early and middle Saxon pottery in the region – precisely when remained unclear. The small, outlying sites had, however, certainly been abandoned by the time Saxo-Norman pottery was introduced, in the second half of the ninth century, after which date occupation was entirely restricted to the areas which, by the thirteenth century, were occupied by villages.[20] In one sense, this new research supported Thirsk, echoing as it did the German evidence on which her model was partly based, for the gradual development, over time, of nucleated villages. But as the open fields of the area had been laid out over the abandoned scattered sites, Hall and Foard began to argue that open-field agriculture itself had originated at the same time as the nucleation 'event', as part of a single 'Great Re-planning' of the landscape, probably directed by kings and lords.[21] That the transformation was, indeed, a planned one was indicated by the apparently 'planned' layout of many Northamptonshire villages – comprising networks of neatly parallel tofts and crofts with both a shared frontage on a road or green, and a shared rear boundary. Planning was also suggested by the arrangement of properties within the fields themselves: holdings – the yardlands or virgates – were often distributed through the fields in a regular sequence, with

18. B.M.S. Campbell, 'Commonfield origins – the regional dimension', in T. Rowley (ed.), *The origins of open-field agriculture* (London, 1981), pp. 112–29; H.S.A. Fox, 'Approaches to the adoption of the Midland system', in T. Rowley (ed.), *The origins of open-field agriculture* (London, 1981), pp. 64–111, at p. 88.

19. G. Foard, 'Systematic fieldwalking and the investigation of Saxon settlement in Northamptonshire', *World Archaeology*, 9 (1978), pp. 357–74.

20. C. Lewis, P. Mitchell-Fox and C. Dyer, *Village, hamlet and field: changing settlements in central England* (Macclesfield, 2002), p. 81; T. Brown and G. Foard, 'The Saxon landscape: a regional perspective', in P. Everson and T. Williamson (eds), *The archaeology of landscape* (Manchester, 1998), pp. 73–82.

21. Brown and Foard, 'Saxon landscape', pp. 67–94; D. Hall, *Medieval fields* (Aylesbury, 1982).

cultivators having the same neighbours in each furlong. There was also, Hall argued, a close relationship between the overall number of virgate holdings in a village, and its hidation assessment as set out in Domesday Book.[22]

While these contributions presented new ideas about agency and chronology, the most important elements of Thirsk's model remained largely intact. In particular, most commentators continued to associate the emergence of open fields (and nucleated villages) with pressure on resources. To Fox, for example, the first regular open fields arose when, because of the fragmentation of large 'multiple estates' in the late Saxon period, communities came to be severed from their traditional grazing lands, experiencing a shortage of grazing which precipitated the kind of reorganisation of formerly less regular field systems envisaged by Thirsk. To David Hall, the principal driving force for change:

> may have been population pressure and the reduction of waste for animals to graze, so necessitating the use of fallow grazing. If there were to be common grazing over fallow arable, then large areas of land would be needed; such an arrangement would be unworkable if, for instance, all the 12 small Saxon settlements at Brixworth tried to operate their own fallow grazing in an unenclosed landscape. The animals from one small area of fallow would trespass on the crops of the neighbouring farms.[23]

Where Thirsk was right: the chronology of common fields

Much of Thirsk's model thus remained intact, but now with a very different chronology, one which implied that population was pressing hard on resources across much of Midland England by the eighth or ninth centuries, rather than four centuries later. This earlier timescale, a significant modification of Thirsk's original model, is now well entrenched in the archaeological and to some extent the historical literature. But was Thirsk in fact so wrong on this point? More recent research, on a number of fronts, has if anything tended to shift common-field genesis forwards in time once again, at least to the eleventh and arguably into the twelfth century.

At the core of this revision lies a new interpretation of the archaeological evidence, which raises questions about whether the nucleation 'event' of the eighth or ninth centuries ever really took place. The impression conveyed in many texts, that most Northamptonshire townships contain a host of abandoned early Saxon settlements, is certainly misleading. A recent reassessment of the Northamptonshire evidence suggests that, in spite of the intensity with which fieldwork has been carried out in Northamptonshire, by Hall especially, over half of the townships in the county (51 per cent) have produced no evidence at all for

---

22. D. Hall, *The open fields of Northamptonshire* (Northampton, 1995), pp. 82–94.
23. Hall, *The open fields of Northamptonshire*, p. 139.

such outlying sites; while only c.4 per cent of townships contain more than three.[24] Excavations in Northamptonshire and elsewhere suggest, moreover, that most early Saxon settlements were comparatively short-lived, the settlement pattern of the fifth, sixth and seventh centuries being characterised by a high degree of mobility.[25] Scattered early Saxon sites, where these exist, must represent to a large extent a pattern of mobile sites, which *stabilised* in the seventh or eighth centuries, rather than a dispersed pattern of settlements, all occupied at the same time and which were suddenly 'nucleated' by lordly intervention or otherwise – a suggestion also supported by the research in the Whittlewood Forest area by Jones and Page. Villages developed gradually, following stabilisation, as these small foci – 'pre-village nuclei', in Jones and Page's terminology – expanded.[26] But they did so in a variety of ways which are to some extent reflected in their plan forms.

In areas of relatively free-draining soils, as in the valley of the Nene, two or occasionally three settlements, lying a few hundred metres apart, expanded and fused to form a 'polyfocal' village, to use Christopher Taylor's term.[27] But on more difficult soils, growth was usually from a single nucleus. Either way, early stages of expansion often led to loose scatters of farms around areas of damp or infertile soils, creating large central 'greens' like those which formed the basis for much settlement in areas outside the Midlands. In Northamptonshire, however, these areas of common grazing were usually infilled with further farms and houses as the population continued to grow, leaving at most only small residual patches of pasture, diminutive 'greens' within settlements, linked by roads.[28] This is a pattern of development that has been noted elsewhere in the Midland counties, and also in parts of northern Europe.[29] In other cases, where soils were lighter and/or more fertile, all the land lying adjacent to the initial Saxon 'cores' was rapidly brought into cultivation, and later settlement was thus obliged to expand across arable land, already divided into strips. It was this, rather than lordly 'planning', which appears to have created the pattern of neatly parallel tofts found in many Northamptonshire villages, and presumably

24. T. Williamson, R. Liddiard and T. Partida, *Champion: the making and unmaking of the English Midland landscape* (Liverpool, 2013), p. 57.
25. A.E. Brown and G. Foard, 'The Anglo-Saxon period', in M.E. Tingle (ed.), *The archaeology of Northamptonshire* (Northampton, 2004), pp. 78–101, at p. 82; H. Hamerow, 'Settlement mobility and the "Middle Saxon Shift": rural settlements and settlement patterns in Anglo-Saxon England', *Anglo-Saxon England*, 20 (1991), pp. 1–17; C. Taylor, *Village and farmstead* (London, 1983), pp. 120–1.
26. R. Jones and M. Page, *Medieval villages in an English landscape: beginnings and ends* (Macclesfield, 2006).
27. C. Taylor, 'Polyfocal settlement and the English village', *Medieval Archaeology*, 21 (1977), pp. 189–93.
28. Williamson *et al.*, *Champion*, pp. 80–3.
29. S. Oosthuizen, 'Ancient greens in Midland landscapes: Barrington, Cambridgeshire', *Medieval Archaeology*, 46 (2002), pp. 110–15; S. Oosthuizen, 'Medieval greens and moats in the Central Province: evidence from the Bourne valley, Cambridgeshire', *Landscape History*, 24 (2002), pp. 73–87; H. Rennes, 'Grainlands: the landscape of open fields in a European perspective', *Landscape History*, 31 (2010), pp. 37–70, at p. 56.

those elsewhere in the Midlands.[30] This is not to deny that some villages may have been 'planned', in whole or part, but these appear to constitute a small minority of apparently 'regular' settlements, at least in Midland counties.

If villages developed gradually, through the later Saxon and into the post-Conquest period, the same must have been true of their fields. Thirsk's essential linkage of common fields and population growth is crucial here. It is simply impossible to believe that anything like as much land was being cultivated by the small settlement foci of the seventh century, as was farmed from the much larger villages that had developed from these by the eleventh or twelfth centuries. There is, more importantly, very little reason to believe that the regular patterns of holdings scattered through the fields recorded in late medieval documents was already in place by the time of Domesday. David Hall's complex calculations supposedly show a relationship between hidation assessments and the number of virgates (or farms) making up these regular tenurial patterns. A more direct approach is perhaps more useful: that is, a simple comparison of the number of yardlands in particular townships with the number of holdings recorded in 1086. This can be done for 58 Northamptonshire townships, and in *every* case there were more late medieval yardlands than Domesday farms – in all but 14 cases, more than twice as many. To take some striking examples: the highly regular arrangement of holdings at Ecton, recorded on a map of 1703, was almost certainly in existence in the thirteenth century, but seems unlikely to have been created before the twelfth century as there were 110 yardlands, yet only 37 Domesday farms; the system at Muscott, set out in a field book of 1433, had 19 yardlands, but that township contained only three holdings at the time of Domesday; while the regular order of 40 yardlands at Mears Ashby cannot date back to the time of Domesday, when there were only 20 farms in the township.[31] This clearly indicates that regular arrangements of holdings, and thus the layout of open fields as we see them in late medieval documents or post-medieval maps, *must* in general date to some period after the Conquest. Harold Fox drew attention, in the 1980s, to two documents which appeared to indicate the remodelling of field systems on new lines, in counties bordering on Northamptonshire – at Dry Drayton in Cambridgeshire and Segenhoe in Bedfordshire – and it is noteworthy that both date from the mid-twelfth century.[32] In short, by the seventh century some form of open-field cultivation appears to have existed in England, in some places at least, and by the tenth extensive areas were occupied by intermixed arable (on the chalklands of southern England especially). However, the regular, complex 'common field' systems – with their even scatter of properties, regulated cropping regimes and the rest – seem to have been a later development, dating in large part to the eleventh or twelfth centuries; a chronology also supported by the archaeological evidence,

30. Williamson *et al.*, *Champion*, pp. 84–7.
31. Williamson *et al.*, *Champion*, pp. 121–2.
32. Fox, 'Approaches to the adoption of the Midland system', pp. 95–8.

discussed by Richard Jones, for changes in manuring patterns, indicated by pottery scatters, in Midland fields for this same period.[33]

This dating of the emergence of 'common fields' is slightly earlier, by perhaps a century, than that advanced by Thirsk. But in essence her chronology was correct, and for the right reasons. The transition to highly regulated types of extensive open field was the outcome of population growth, of pressure on grazing resources especially, and must therefore have occurred earlier, rather than later, in the development of medieval settlements.

Where Thirsk was mistaken

While Joan Thirk's general explanation for the development of common-field systems appears to have stood the test of time, with even her proposed chronology now seemingly confirmed by recent research, some aspects of her theory appear today less easy to sustain, and her mistakes in this respect arguably arose, at least in part, from a failure to recognise the full implications of her own model. Thirsk's argument that common fields had developed gradually, from less regular systems, was also used to explain why they failed to develop in many parts of the country. Areas with less 'regular' field systems and dispersed patterns of settlement were, she believed, arrested stages of development: they were found in more 'pastoral', less populous districts, where communities never came to experience the crisis of resources which obliged their fellows in the central areas of England to reorganise their farming along more 'regular' lines.[34] But there are many problems with such an interpretation. Given, as we have seen, that common fields were probably developing out of less regular arrangements in the eleventh and twelfth centuries, we might reasonably expect to see some correlation at a national scale between their distribution and the relative densities of plough teams and population recorded by Domesday Book in 1086. While it is true that this source has important distortions and biases, the complete absence of any correlation is striking.[35] If anything, the most intensively ploughed and most populous regions were characterised by dispersed forms of settlement and by fields which deviated in various ways from the fully developed systems which were Thirsk's key concern.

Moreover, while many places in which common fields developed were indeed characterised by intensively arable landscapes, with little grazing land, by the twelfth or thirteenth centuries, as the model requires, this was by no means always the case. In areas of light land – on chalk or sand – significant reserves of pasture often remained throughout the middle ages because these formed an integral part of the arable farming system. They provided the grazing for the large folding flocks without which the

---

33. R. Jones, 'Signatures in the soil: the use of pottery in manure scatters in the identification of medieval arable farming regimes', *Archaeological Journal*, 161 (2005), pp. 159–88.
34. Thirsk, 'The common fields', pp. 24–5.
35. H.C. Darby, *Domesday England* (Cambridge, 1973).

thin, easily leached soils could not have been kept in permanent cultivation – as well as allowing farmers to produce meat and wool for the market. On the chalklands of Wessex or the South Downs, extensive and highly regulated open fields, containing the intermixed strips of many farmers and cultivated from nucleated villages, could be found interspersed with vast tracts of unploughed downland. Even in the Midlands, pasture was often surprisingly extensive. Historians studying open fields in Northamptonshire usually concentrate their attention on areas such as the Nene valley, where, by the high middle ages, landscapes of almost unrelieved arable had indeed developed. But in the west of the county equally regular field systems, farmed from equally nucleated villages, are found, with numerous broad bands of unploughed ground, managed as pasture or meadow, interspersed with the furlongs. In some of these townships no more than half the land area was under cultivation. Given that most such places followed a two-course rotation, less than a quarter of their land would have been under crops each year.[36] The converse is also true: areas of 'irregular' field systems were not necessarily thinly settled landscapes geared primarily towards livestock production. On the poor, heavy soils of the London clays around London, for example, 'the pre-eminence of enclosed land did not mean that the economy was based primarily on pastoral or woodland activities ... it was not until the second half of the fourteenth centuries that the larger farmers on the London Clay began to adopt the pastoral bias for which they were later famous'.[37] In East Anglia, dispersed settlement, enclosures and irregular open fields were associated with a densely populated landscape, in which most of the land area was under the plough.[38] Although such arrangements also characterised sparsely settled, largely pastoral areas, as in parts of the west Midlands,[39] it is probably true to say that areas with, and without, common fields could both be found in areas in which population densities attained high, medium and low levels.

Settlements and fields

One explanation for this apparent conundrum is implied in a seldom noticed feature of Thirsk's own model. The extensive but chaotic intermixture of strips, which presumably existed before field systems were regularised, is most likely to have arisen in situations where farmers were unwilling or unable to move away from an existing settlement as population grew and the frontiers of cultivation expanded. In such circumstances, where farms were being divided by inheritance – or where property was being allotted to sub-tenants, freed slaves or otherwise subject to some form of equitable division – then sub-division of individual parcels

36. T. Williamson, *Environment, society and landscape in early medieval England* (Woodbridge, 2013), pp. 147–50.
37. D. Roden, 'Field systems of the Chilterns and their environs', in A.R.H. Baker and R.A. Butlin (eds), *Studies of field systems in the British Isles* (Cambridge, 1973), pp. 325–76, at p. 341.
38. M. Bailey, *Medieval Suffolk: an economic and social history 1200–1500* (Woodbridge, 2007).
39. C. Dyer, 'Dispersed settlements in medieval England: a case study of Pendock, Worcestershire', *Medieval Archaeology*, 34 (1990), pp. 97–121.

(rather than allocation of integral parcels) was likely to result in order to provide an equal share of land near to, and away from, the settlement. This was important not only to allow equal ease of access at crucial points in the farming year, but also because land nearer the settlement was likely to have received more manure, carted out from yards and middens, and thus likely to be more fertile. Where, in contrast, farmers were able to migrate more easily from existing settlement sites, then the extent of intermixture, as population grew and the frontiers of cultivation expanded, would of necessity have been less. Thirsk failed to discuss in any detail the close relationship which existed between field systems and settlement patterns. But that association forms, nevertheless, an important if not central feature of her model. Only where settlement remained nucleated, and failed to disperse across the landscape, would extensive and continuous areas of intermixed arable, containing the lands of large numbers of cultivators, have developed – which could then be reorganised, in the manner described, along more 'regular' lines. Looked at in this way, the logic of Thirsk's model implies that regional variations in the character of field systems need to be interpreted, at least in part, in terms of regional variations in the development of early medieval settlement patterns.

There is no room here to discuss in any detail why, in some districts, farms remained clustered as the population grew, while in others they spread out across the landscape: these are matters which I have addressed elsewhere.[40] Suffice it to say that people congregated in villages mainly as a consequence of environmental factors. As noted, a number of historians before Thirsk – most notably the Orwins – had emphasised the importance of 'co-aration' in the genesis of open fields, noting that sharing of ploughs and teams amongst peasant farmers was common practice in early medieval England.[41] As larger and heavier ploughs came into widespread use in the course of the Saxon period, cultivators might have been encouraged to live in close proximity in order to facilitate sharing, in circumstances where assembly of teams had to be carried out with particular rapidity – something difficult to achieve where farms were scattered widely across the landscape. In this context, the close association of villages and common fields, and pre-Cretaceous clays and mudstones in Midland counties giving rise to particularly difficult soils – *pelostagnogleys* or non-calcareous *pelosols* – should be noted. Such soils are especially prone to structural damage when ploughed wet, a fact which would have placed a premium on the careful timing of agricultural operations, and in particular on the rapid exploitation of ploughing 'windows' during the spring.[42] In addition, co-aration and a particularly short 'window' for cultivation may have had a *direct* impact on the form of fields, encouraging in particular the highly regular scattering of holdings

40. Williamson, *Environment, society and landscape*, pp. 184–206.
41. Orwin and Orwin, *The open fields*, pp. 12–14 and 51–2.
42. Williamson, *Environment, society and landscape*, pp. 196–201; C.A.H. Hodge et al., *Soils and their use in eastern England* (Harpenden, 1984), pp. 155–8; 186–92; 285–8; 293–6 and 351–4.

across land of varying aspect and drainage potential, and lying at varying distances from the village. Ploughed in sequence, the lands of all those who contributed to the common ploughs had an equal likelihood of being ready for seeding in reasonable time and reasonable condition. Other bottlenecks in the farming year, where tools and labour needed to be mobilised with rapidity, may have similarly encouraged a greater degree of settlement clustering in some areas of England than in others. Common fields and villages are often associated with landscapes in which large and continuous areas of meadow land occur,[43] perhaps reflecting the fact that hay needed to be cut, repeatedly turned, carted and stacked with great speed. Poor weather could ruin the harvest, and efficiencies in the organisation of labour, and arising from the sharing of carts and other equipment, would have speeded the effective execution of these tasks. And in areas of light, freely draining soils – generally characterised in both England and France by nucleated villages and forms of 'common field' – the critical need to replenish nutrients lost through leaching put a particular premium on the 'close folding' of sheep on the arable. As farms increasingly developed as collections of intermixed, unhedged strips this was best achieved through the development of communal flocks and rotations, most easily administered from a clustered group of farms.

In addition to any specifically *agricultural* incentives for proximate living, there were probably other factors, most importantly water supply. Over much of England water can be obtained almost anywhere from shallow wells, but in areas of very permeable geology, such as chalk and limestone; and also across much of the Midlands, where pre-Cretaceous clays form deep impermeable masses, without significant aquifers; good supplies of water tend to be found only at spring and seepage lines. Although more than one possible site for settlement was usually available, hydrological circumstances certainly seem to have contributed to the clustering of settlement, in combination with the kinds of agrarian imperative already described. And it was this clustering which, in the final analysis, arguably created the *extensively* intermixed properties out of which Thirsk's more regular 'common fields' were fashioned.

Conclusion

It is hard to exaggerate the importance of Joan Thirsk's contribution to the debates about open-field origins. Her ideas regarding the gradual development of 'regular' field systems, and especially the suggestion that they arose primarily from population growth and pressure on resources, remain extremely influential. While some aspects of her model have been questioned over the last four decades, recent research has often tended to support her views, on the chronology of common-fields especially. And like all the best models in history, even its shortcomings encourage – as this short account has hopefully demonstrated – new ways of thinking about a debate which remains of central importance in landscape history.

---

43. B.M.S. Campbell, *English seigniorial agriculture* (Cambridge, 2006), pp. 75–6.

6

A 'countrie' consisting wholly of woodland, 'bredd of Oxen and Dairies'? Agricultural regions and rural communities in lowland pastoral Shropshire during the early modern period

JAMES P. BOWEN

The definition of farming regions by Thirsk, which built on pioneering work by Darby and Hoskins, marked one of her most significant contributions, highlighting variations in agriculture and rural society. It was an important step forward in English local history, and had implications for those working on past economies, societies and cultures.[1] Everitt developed the application of the French geographical concept of 'pays' in which landscapes were seen as having a social and cultural dimension.[2] The model of agricultural or farming regions and 'pays' has been widely adopted since by early modern historians working on, for example, Civil War allegiance, riot and popular protest.[3] This chapter reviews Thirsk's view of farming regions with reference to Shropshire as an example of a county which contained a variety of contrasting regions or 'pays' including corn-growing vales to the south-east, and large areas of both wood-pasture and open pasture. Through the analysis of probate inventories for the parish of Prees and work by other researchers, it seeks to reaffirm the regional approach, whilst pointing out that this interpretative framework needs to take into account small sub-regions, and the activities, both agricultural and industrial, of everyone in rural communities.

1. H.C. Darby, 'Some early ideas on the agricultural regions of England', *Agricultural History Review*, 2 (1954), pp. 30–47; W.G. Hoskins, 'Regional farming in England', *Agricultural History Review*, 2 (1954), pp. 3–11; J. Thirsk (ed.), *The agrarian history of England and Wales* (hereafter AHEW), 4: 1500–1640 (Cambridge, 1967), pp. 1–112.
2. A.M. Everitt, 'Reflections on the historical origin of regions and pays', *Journal of Historical Geography*, 3.1 (1977), pp. 1–19.
3. D. Underdown, *Revel, riot and rebellion: popular politics and culture in England 1603–1660* (Oxford, 1985).

Farming regions 1500 - 1640

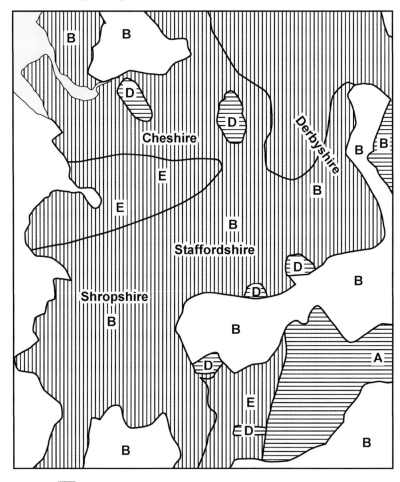

Mixed Farming types
B   Corn and stock variously combined (in clay vales)

Pasture Farming Types

Open Pasture
B   Rearing and fattening
E   Dairying

Wood Pasture
A   Dairying and pig keeping, sometimes with horse-breeding
B   Stock-keeping with corn-growing, sometimes with dairying
D   Stock-rearing and pig-keeping, sometimes with horse-breeding

Figure 6.1 Map of Thirsk's farming regions of Shropshire for 1500–1640 and 1640–1750
Note: See the amalgamation of the two pastoral types (wood-pasture and open pasture).
Source: Thirsk (ed.), *AHEW*, 4, p. 4; *AHEW*, 5, part 1, p. 131.

Farming regions 1640 - 1750

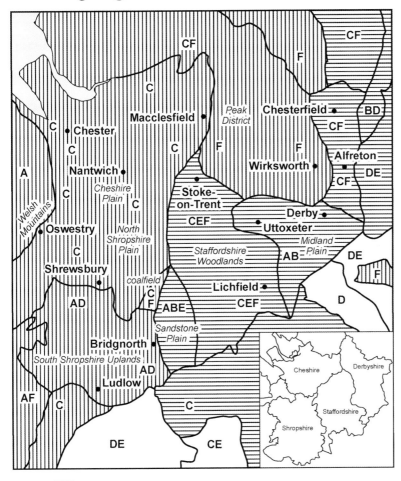

Pastoral types
A   Subsistence corn with cattle rearing and sheep keeping
C   Subsistence corn with cattle rearing, dairying and/or grazing
D   Cattle grazing
E   Dairying
F   Subsistence corn with stock and industries

Intermediate types
A   Corn and sheep
B   Corn and cattle with substantial rearing side
C   Corn and cattle with substantial dairying side
D   Corn and cattle with substantial feeding side
E   Corn and cattle with other enterprises
F   Corn and livestock (sometimes including dairying)
     with industries

Arable types
D   Corn and cattle with substantial feeding
E   Corn and livestock with special enterprises,
     eg horses, pigs, fruit, hops, vegetables, dye crops

Thirsk's view of Shropshire

In terms of farming regions, Thirsk labelled Shropshire as a county of 'open pasture', characterised by 'rearing and fattening' with 'dairying' in the north.[4] In addition to the evidence of probate inventories, with their details of crops and livestock, contemporary comment influences the definition of farming regions. Sir Thomas Coningsby (d.1625), Member of Parliament for Herefordshire, described Shropshire as a 'Countrie' consisting wholly of woodland, 'bredd of Oxen & Dairie's w[hi]ch if they were pulled downe, it would breed a great scarcitie amongst the people there, then the scarcitie of Corne nowe is'.[5] This consideration helped to exclude the county from the act in 1597 to restore land recently converted to pasture back to the cultivation of corn.[6] Thirsk's emphasis on the importance of livestock farming is broadly correct, however, it over-simplifies the county's varieties of landscapes. She later refined this regional framework and saw a greater degree of sub-division which took into consideration not just farming practice, but also the growth of rural industry which she associated with pastoral regions. In addition, in her view specialisation increased in the period 1640–1750 as agriculture became more commercialised (Figure 6.1).[7]

Much research on the agrarian history of England undertaken in the 1970s and 1980s was based on the quantitative analysis of probate inventories which were seen as documenting the growth in the intensity of the pastoral farming economy in Shropshire. Edwards used inventories to reveal the number of cattle and sheep kept by an emerging group of yeoman graziers in different regions, taking samples from the 1550s, the 1660s and the 1740s. On the north Shropshire plain the median cattle herds for the three decades numbered 9–10, 9 and 18–19, respectively. The comparable figures for the Severn-Tern and Weald Moors were 11, 11 and 16; for the heathlands 11, 7–9 and 12–15; and on the eastern sandstone plain 7, 8–9 and 12.[8] In all of these regions, the numbers were relatively high, and rose decisively between the mid-seventeenth and mid-eighteenth centuries.

4. J. Thirsk, *England's agricultural regions and agrarian history, 1500–1750* (London, 1987), p. 28.
5. A.F. Pollard and M. Blatcher, 'Hayward Townshend's Journals', *Bulletin of the Institute of Historical Research*, 12 (1934–5), p. 16; P.E.J. Hammer, 'Coningsby, Sir Thomas (1550–1625)', *Oxford Dictionary of National Biography* (Oxford, 2004); online edn, January 2008 <http://www.oxforddnb.com/view/article/6075>, accessed July 2015.
6. *An act for the maintenance of husbandry and tillage* (1598).
7. Thirsk (ed.), *AHEW, 5: 1640–1750, part 1 regional farming systems* (Cambridge, 1984); J. Thirsk, 'Industries in the countryside', in J. Thirsk, *The rural economy of England: collected essays* (London, 1984), pp. 217–33.
8. P.R. Edwards, 'The farming economy of north east Shropshire in the seventeenth century' (DPhil thesis, Oxford, 1976); P.R. Edwards, '1540–1750', in G.C. Baugh (ed.), *VCH: Shropshire, 4, Agriculture* (Oxford, 1989), pp. 119–68.

In particular Edwards highlighted the significance of the north Shropshire dairy industry.[9]

Thus a series of farming sub-regions was identified. On the lowland heathlands, meres and mosses of the broad north Shropshire plain, farmers were primarily engaged in 'subsistence corn with cattle rearing, dairying, and/ or grazing'.[10] Kerridge noted this 'Cheshire cheese country' attracted comments from contemporaries, notably Daniel Defoe (1660–1731) who, in the 1720s, wrote that 'great quantities of it [Cheshire cheese] are made in Shropshire, Staffordshire, and Lancashire'.[11] Thirsk pointed out that dairying – a form of 'alternative agriculture' – emerged in the mid-seventeenth century with increasing demand during the Civil War and from industrial populations.[12] It grew in importance in the national market in the post-Restoration period, with greater specialisation of traditional dairying regions and their geographical enlargement. Dairy farming developed with the improvement of waste and piecemeal enclosure of common fields. This enabled new farms to be created and existing holdings to expand, providing greater pasturage. Samuel Garbet (1685–1756), a local antiquary, wrote in his *History of Wem*, written around *c*.1750, that the pastures and meadows of North Bradford Hundred

> generally produce good grass and hay, and thereby maintain great dairies, which supply the markets with plenty of butter, and the factors with vast quantities of cheese, in goodness not much inferior to those of Cheshire.[13]

Other farming sub-regions of Shropshire reflected their physical characteristics. The predominantly upland south of the county, encompassing the Shropshire Hills, Clun Forest and the Clee Hills in the late seventeenth and early eighteenth centuries was classified by Thirsk as 'subsistence corn with cattle rearing and sheep keeping' and 'cattle grazing'.[14] In the south Shropshire hill country, communities with common rights drove their livestock, mainly cattle, sheep and pigs, along 'straker' routes known as 'driftways' or 'outracks' that led to commons such as Clee Forest, Clun Forest, the Long Mynd and the Stiperstones,

9. P.R. Edwards, 'The development of dairy farming of the north Shropshire plain in the seventeenth century', *Midland History*, 4 (1977), pp. 175–90.

10. Thirsk (ed.), *AHEW*, 5, part 1, p. 131.

11. E. Kerridge, *The agricultural revolution* (London, 1967), pp. 129–31; D. Defoe, *A tour through England and Wales*, 2 (London, 1963), p. 72; Thirsk, *England's agricultural regions*, p. 24.

12. J. Thirsk, 'Agricultural policy: public debate and legislation', *AHEW*, 5, part 2, *Agrarian change* (Cambridge, 1984), pp. 328, 361–3; J. Thirsk, *Alternative agriculture: a history from the black death to the present day* (Oxford, 2000), pp. 166–7; Thirsk, *England's agricultural regions*, p. 18.

13. S. Garbet, *History of Wem and the following villages and townships, viz. Edstaston Cotton, Lowe and Ditches, Horton, Newtown, Wolverley, Northwood, Tilley, Sleap, Aston and Lacon* (Wem, 1818), p. 8.

14. Thirsk (ed.), *AHEW*, 5, part 1, p. 131.

which had pastoral management practices reflecting their earlier forest status and distinctive upland character.[15]

By contrast, in the same period the eastern sandstone plain bordering south Staffordshire and north Worcestershire, where the soil was light and thin, was characterised by Thirsk as an intermediate sub-region whose farming was 'corn and sheep', 'corn and cattle with substantial rearing' and 'corn and cattle with other enterprises' – essentially 'corn country'.[16] It also included Morfe, a royal forest or common as it was known following disafforestation, which was an extensive wood-pasture area on the fringe of open pasture and arable land. Consequently, this provided potential for the inclusion of both extensive open-field cultivation and large heaths and commons within husbandry practices. That part of the county east of the river Severn had traditionally been known, as Tanner remarked in the mid-nineteenth century, as 'the Wheatlands', resembling the 'classic' arable-orientated commercialising agricultural regions of midland, southern and eastern England. Thirsk, looking at evidence before 1750, noted its sheep–corn economy, but with rye as its major crop.[17] Probate inventories for Claverley parish, located in the eastern sandstone plain, give the impression that the pastoral sheep–corn farming economy provided a living for a group of wealthy yeomen who kept as many as 200 or 300 sheep, whilst small and medium-sized farmers owned flocks of between 30 and 50.[18]

The Weald Moors, an area of low-lying fen, marsh and moor located in north-east Shropshire, prior to enclosure and improvement in the nineteenth century had a typical fenland economy. This wetland landscape was comparable to the Lincolnshire Fens which had been studied by Thirsk, but she did not pick out the Weald Moors as deserving special mention in her survey of the Shropshire farming regions. Pastoralism was combined with fishing, fowling and the exploitation of other natural resources, with only limited arable cultivation, giving rise to a specialised form of husbandry and a traditional way of life.[19] In the eighteenth century the antiquarian and clergyman George Plaxton (1647/8–1720)

---

15. For studies of upland pastoral economies see T. Rowley, 'The Clee Forest – A Study in Common Rights', *Transactions of the Shropshire Archaeological and Historical Society*, 58 (1965–8), pp. 48–67; A.J.L. Winchester, *The harvest of the hills: rural life in northern England and the Scottish borders 1400–1700* (Edinburgh, 2000); H.S.A. Fox, *Dartmoor's alluring uplands: transhumance and pastoral management in the middle ages* (Exeter, 2011).

16. Thirsk (ed.), *AHEW*, 5, part I, p. 131.

17. H. Tanner, 'The agriculture of Shropshire', *Journal of the Royal Agricultural Society of England*, 19 (1858), pp. 1–65, especially p. 7; Thirsk (ed.), *AHEW*, 5, part I, p. 156.

18. Shropshire Archives (hereafter SA), Shrewsbury, q OJ 55.5.

19. Thirsk, *English peasant farming*, pp. 27–36, 110; P.R. Edwards, 'Competition for land, common rights and drainage in the Weald Moors (Shropshire): the Cherrington and Meeson disputes, 1576–1612' in R.W. Hoyle (ed.), *People, landscape and alternative agriculture: essays for Joan Thirsk* (Exeter, 2004), pp. 39–55.

noted the waterlogged character of the district, and traced it back to the remote period when place-names were formed, interpreting Eyton as the 'Town upon the Waters', Adeney as 'Edwyney, Edwin's Island', and Buttery as 'Buttery the island of Butter, being a long Grazing Tract of Land'.[20] Also distinguishable, with the emergence of early industry in the Severn Gorge and the east Shropshire coalfield, was a small pastoral industrial region described by Thirsk as 'subsistence corn with cattle rearing, dairying, and/or grazing' and 'subsistence corn with stock and industries'.[21] Further topographical sub-division can be made between the north-western meres and mosses, the north-eastern heathlands, the south and central Shropshire plain, lowland areas surrounding the uplands of south Shropshire and lower-lying river valley land such as Corvedale.

Interpreting farming regions

The mapping of farming regions has done much to inform our understanding, but how do we move beyond an interpretation of rural England in terms of agricultural or farming regions, sub-regions and '*pays*'? In light of subsequent research, in what ways should Thirsk's ideas, and those of other historians writing in the light of her approach be revised and modified? Little or no attempt has been made to update or redraw Thirsk's definitive map of farming regions. Even within the sub-regions of Shropshire a variety of smaller units can be identified, and it may be that a concern to recognise regions has been concealing small-scale local differences. Early modern social historians have focused their attention on the 'politics of the parish' and this approach has explored the importance of agrarian communities' resistance to landlords and challenges to custom at village level.[22] In the same way, at the bottom of the hierarchy of farming regions, sub-regions and '*pays*' is the manor and parish, or even, in some parts of England, the hamlet or township. No two manors and parishes were the same, and even within them there could be a variety of landscapes, farming practices and a range of rural crafts and industries, as well as different forms of manorial or parochial organisation. Parishes could be arable or pastoral, enclosed or unenclosed, 'open' or 'closed', agricultural or industrial – each presents us with a variety of economic, social, cultural, political and religious characteristics. This is particularly applicable to transitional woodland areas which were far from uniform. Farming regions and sub-regions were made up of constituent manors, parishes, hamlets and townships and even individual farms as Overton implied, and therefore, research can be concentrated on very small units of agricultural activity. Parochial studies

20. G. Plaxton, 'Some natural observations made in the parishes of Kinardsey and Donington in Shropshire', *Philosophical Transactions*, 25 (1706–7), pp. 2418–23.
21. Thirsk (ed.), *AHEW*, 5, part 1, p. 131.
22. K. Wrightson, 'The politics of the parish in early modern England', in P. Griffiths, A. Fox and S. Hindle (eds), *The experience of authority in early modern England* (London, 1996), pp. 10–46.

can still have a place in schemes of agrarian history that recognise the importance of regions.[23]

Naturally the focus of historians has been on those wealthy gentry, yeoman farmers and husbandmen whose activities are most fully documented and formed the basis of samples used by Thirsk and others to identify the agricultural specialisation of regions. Probate inventories for Myddle parish in north Shropshire reveal that the farming economy was concentrated on livestock production with the average number of cattle being 13.7 (15.1 including oxen), 9 (10 including oxen) and 13.4 for the periods 1551–1600, 1600–40 and 1664–1701 respectively.[24] The importance of dairy farming is apparent with two in every five cattle being milk cows, and as their numbers grew there was a reduction in the size of sheep flocks. This contrasts with Shawbury where there appears to have been no dramatic change in the average number of cattle, cows or other livestock between 1538 and 1725 although there was a small rise in sheep farming.[25]

Smallholders and industrial workers

Analysis of probate inventories at the individual parish level provides insight into not only the importance of pastoral pursuits, but also the increasing economic and social polarisation in rural communities. Communities ranged from wealthy gentry and yeoman farmers to smaller farmers, husbandmen and smallholders, as well as those inhabitants employed in craft and industrial occupations and, of course, the poor. It is necessary to include these lesser people in the analysis in order to encompass the agricultural activities of all those within a community, and to make the connection between the farming economy of a region and the myriad of domestic or household economies.

Probate inventories tended to be compiled for the better-off, and consequently those that are available for historians to analyse are a socially biased sample. The inclusion of the inventories of craftsmen, labourers and tradesmen, when they survive, gives a more accurate impression of the farming of the whole community, as the less affluent were still active in the economy and had some cumulative importance because they were numerous. As Muldrew's work has shown, labourers might have kept their own livestock, grown crops and worked at a craft or trade.[26] In her work on Eccleshall, a large multi-township parish in north Staffordshire, described in detail by Gregory King (1648–1712), Spufford itemised different types

23. M. Overton, 'Agricultural regions in early modern England: an example from East Anglia', Department of Geography, University of Newcastle upon Tyne (1988); M. Overton, *The agricultural revolution in England: the transformation of the agrarian economy 1500–1850* (Cambridge, 1996), pp. 46–62.
24. D.G. Hey, *An English rural community: Myddle under the Tudors and Stuarts* (Leicester, 1974), pp. 57–70.
25. R. Collingwood, *Shawbury: the people and how they lived 1538–1725* (Longaston, 2011), pp. 47–64.
26. C. Muldrew, *Food, energy and the creation of industriousness: work and material culture in agrarian England, 1550–1780* (Cambridge, 2011), pp. 246–59.

of inhabitants who included dairymen and dairy wives producing cheese for the London market, as well as a large numbers of labourers, cottagers, encroachers, craftsmen and poor who settled in the parish, often on unenclosed commons.[27] Commercialised agriculture was not, therefore, practised by all the farms and land holdings in a parish or region. This parish exemplifies a 'horn and thorn' farming economy, which Thirsk illustrated with reference to Staffordshire as containing a greater extent of waste than open-field 'champion' landscapes, and having in its lowlands a strong tendency to pastoralism.[28] Moreover, she argued for an understanding of pastoral husbandry in order to explain how England changed from a predominantly rural–agrarian to a largely urban–industrial society.

Prees, a large multi-township parish in north Shropshire similar in many respects to Eccleshall, had extensive areas of heathland and woodland commons. Analysis of surviving probate inventories reveals the presence of large dairy farmers often cited as exemplars of agricultural specialisation, reaffirming Thirsk's and Edwards's model for the county and region.[29] They kept large herds of cows typically numbering between 20 and 30, as well as calves and heifers and a bull, and they maintained dairying apparatus, such as cheese presses and tubs, and a quantity of cheese in store. Also, they each had a sizeable flock of between 40 and 150 sheep, kept a number of pigs and cropped considerable acreages which significantly added to their wealth. The link between dairying and pig-keeping was raised by Thirsk because whilst in the medieval period woodlands were used for grazing pigs, pigs were also kept by dairymen who fed them on whey and fattened them on beans and peas.[30] In the mid-eighteenth century Garbet noted that Shropshire hogs were 'reckoned the best in England, and those of North Bradford [hundred] as good as any in the county; they are large, broad set, and weighty, which may be owing to their being fed with peas'.[31] Therefore inventory evidence for the agricultural activities of these wealthy gentry, yeoman farmers and husbandmen confirms the conventional view of the farming system of the north Shropshire plain. However, their activities starkly contrast with the majority of those who left an inventory and were engaged in small-scale farming, or who were scarcely involved in agriculture

27. M. Spufford and J. Went, *Poverty portrayed: Gregory King and the parish of Eccleshall* (Keele, 1995); M. Spufford, 'Eccleshall, Staffordshire: a bishop's estate of dairy wives, and the poor', in J. Thirsk (ed.), *Rural England: an illustrated history of the landscape* (Oxford, 2000), pp. 290–306. For cottage settlement and encroachment on commons see J.P. Bowen, 'Cottage settlement and encroachment on common waste: some evidence from Shropshire', *Local Population Studies*, 93 (2014), pp. 11–32.
28. J. Thirsk, 'Horn and thorn in Staffordshire: the economy of a pastoral county', in J. Thirsk, *The rural economy of England: collected essays* (London, 1984), pp. 163–82.
29. Lichfield Record Office, Lichfield (hereafter LRO) P/C/11 Prees peculiar court. A total of 458 probate inventories have been consulted.
30. Thirsk, *Alternative agriculture*, p. 49.
31. Garbet, *Wem*, p. 9.

at all. This is in accord with Shaw-Taylor's interpretation of rural society in general in the eighteenth century as being polarised between wealthy farmers and the labourers who often did not keep a single cow.[32]

Generally craftsmen, labourers, tradesmen, spinsters and widows, a high proportion of whom resided in the poorer parts of the parish, namely Prees Higher and Lower Heaths, Calverhall and Whixall, kept a cow or two, a pig, a horse or mare and, in some cases, a small number of sheep which were probably pastured on the unenclosed heathland and woodland commons. Industrial crops such as hemp and flax were widely cultivated and a few grew a small acreage of crops or picked fruit such as apples.[33] In addition to these varied agricultural and horticultural pursuits, some were also involved, like their wealthier neighbours, in dairying, but in their case on such a small scale that it was presumably for household consumption rather than for sale. Crafts and trades are in some cases recorded, including participation in textile manufacture as spinners and weavers of wool, hemp and flax.[34] One inventory of 1742 lists a little pig and a parcel of hay, another (of James Shocklidge in 1669) had two pigs as his sole livestock. A little black cow was the only animal owned by John Brooke in 1712, and he also had some dairying equipment – a churn. Three women who died in 1710, 1712 and 1712 had no livestock, but all were in possession of spinning wheels. There were also those who left no inventory and remain unrecorded. Prees was located in a woodland area where livestock breeding/rearing and dairying were prevalent, the open fields were subject to early enclosure, and extensive commons survived, supporting a large population of smallholders and labourers who worked for wages. It thus displayed many characteristics of the 'semi-farming, semi-industrial communities' defined by Thirsk where 'industries in the countryside' developed.[35] The inventory evidence of cottagers, wage-earners and industrial workers, where it is available, needs to be more fully integrated into the analysis of regional farming systems.

Prees was by no means an isolated example, as the probate inventories show for the parishes of Dawley, Lilleshall, Wellington and Wrockwardine in the area where the heathlands, Weald Moors, and East Shropshire coalfield converge. They indicate that a large number of testators combined farming with another

---

32. L. Shaw-Taylor, 'Access to land in eighteenth century England', in B.J.P. van Bavel and P.C.M. Hoppenbrouwers (eds), *Landholding and land transfer in the North Sea area (late middle ages–19th century)*, CORN publication series 5 (Turnhout, 2004), pp. 265–81. For cow keeping see L. Shaw-Taylor, 'Labourers, cows, common rights and parliamentary enclosure: the evidence of contemporary comment c.1760–1810', *Past and Present*, 171 (2001), pp. 95–126.

33. Thirsk, *Alternative agriculture*, p. 46.

34. Occupations recorded include baker, blacksmith, butcher, carpenter, cooper, cupboard maker, felt maker, gardener, innkeeper, milner, sawer, shingler, tanner, tailor, victualler, weaver and wheelwright. J. Thirsk, *Economic policy and projects: the development of a consumer society in early modern England* (Oxford, 1978).

35. Thirsk, 'Industries in the countryside', p. 231.

occupation as colliers, weavers, miners or blacksmiths.[36] As at Prees, whilst cheese was made by most people for domestic consumption, larger quantities were produced for the market by farmers in Lilleshall and Wrockwardine reflecting large farm sizes and the higher quality of land. In general, herd sizes of both dairy cows and cattle increased after 1660. At Dawley farmers with access to better quality land kept sheep flocks, although these were not as sizeable as those in south Shropshire.

Open fields and enclosure

In seeking to characterise farming regions or sub-regions historians have tended to underestimate the extent of arable land in pastoral areas of England. Shropshire, along with other woodland counties, has been viewed as a county of 'ancient', 'early' or 'old' enclosure which did not develop the open-field systems characteristic of the Midland counties. Hence, contemporaries saw the county as being 'heavily enclosed' along with Herefordshire, Sussex, Suffolk, Somerset, Dorset and parts of Northumberland and North Yorkshire. In the early modern period contemporaries described Shropshire as having an essentially pastoral farming economy, but they also emphasised arable production.[37] In the 1540s John Leland (1503–52) noted the variation in arable, pasture and woodland around the county town Shrewsbury, referring to 'metely good ground, corne and grasse'. In 1612 it was observed that Shropshire's soil was 'rich, and standeth upon a reddish clay, abounding in wheat and barley',[38] whilst in 1673 Shropshire was, according to Richard Blome (1635–1705) 'abounding in wheat and barley' with its pasture feeding 'store of cattle'.[39] In 1652, Walter Blith (1605–54) described Shropshire, along with Warwickshire, Staffordshire, Derbyshire, Yorkshire and 'all the Countries thereabouts, and all the Chalk Counties both south and west', as 'woodland', which until enclosure 'were wonnt to be releeved by the Fieldon with Corne of all sorts, And now are grown as gallant Corne Countries as be in England'.[40] In short, they had lost their 'woodland' character and increased their proportion of arable.

The fields of Shropshire produced a range of crops, notably barley, rye and wheat. However, by the late sixteenth century, population pressure meant that corn had to be imported as Coningsby's reference to the 'scarcitie of corne'

36. B. Trinder and J. Cox, *Yeomen and colliers in Telford: probate inventories for Wellington, Wrockwardine, Lilleshall and Dawley* (Chichester, 1980), pp. 72–90.
37. W. Harrison, *The description of England*, ed. G. Edelen (New York, 1968); J. Aubrey, *The natural history of Wiltshire*, ed. J. Britton (London, 1847), pp. 11–12.
38. L. Toulmin Smith (ed.), *Leland's itinerary in England and Wales* (London, 1906), 2, pp. 81–4; J. Speed, *England, Wales, Scotland, and Ireland described* (1627), Chapter 35.
39. R. Blome, *Britannia* (London, 1673), p. 192.
40. W. Blith, *The English improver improved or the survey of husbandry surveyed discovering the improueableness of all lands: some to be under a double and treble others under a five or six fould. And many under a ten fould, yea some under a twenty fould improvement. By Wa: Blith a lover of ingenuity* (London, 1652), p. 82.

implies. The chronicles of Shrewsbury frequently describe fluctuations in prices, such as the statement in June and July 1585 when 'corne grewe to be verey deare in most places in Englaund … namely in the towne of Salop wheate was at 8s. 8d. the bushell and rye at 6s the bushell'.[41] During times of dearth, scarcity and plague, commons and wastes were cultivated temporarily and the lack of hay and fodder had implications for livestock production. In 1590–1, the high cost of hay and fodder caused 'many cattell to perrishe for waunt'.[42] In districts where there were open fields, exchange by agreement and piecemeal enclosure often undermined the system of communal agriculture in the sixteenth and seventeenth centuries. At Church Aston, near the market town of Newport, a three-field system operated when it was surveyed in 1681–2.[43] Beyond the furlongs were the enclosed areas of meadow, moorland and woodland, and some of the open-field land had been newly enclosed. There were also open fields at Wroxeter shown on an estate map produced by John Rocque (1709–62) in 1747.[44] Clearly, despite not being recognised as an area of 'classic' open-field farming, most villages and townships did in fact have some form of open-field system, although it amounted to a supplementary element in the pastoral farming economy which relied on commons and wastes, but also increasingly on enclosed pasture fields.

The most reliable literary sources for the rural economy of north Shropshire parishes are the descriptions provided by contemporaries who resided in the area, rather than those visitors who associated Shropshire with other parts of England. Formerly 'beautified with many famous woods', Richard Gough (1635–1723) noted the use of common wastes for sheep and cattle grazing, and, in the case of Myddle Wood, its piecemeal enclosure with clearance of vegetation by axe and fire for the cultivation of corn and barley during times of dearth.[45] He recalled the unsuccessful cultivation of Myddle Wood during the Civil War, writing that the common 'was cutt, and burnt, and sowed with corne, which was a very strong crop', although 'the next was a crop of barley, which was soe poore, that most of it was pulled up by the roote, because it was too short to bee cutt'.[46] Nevertheless, comparing the production of crops and livestock of different parishes in the locality he noted: 'This parish [Myddle] yields great plenty of corne, especially of the best barley, which is little inferior to the barley that is gott in Wroxeter fields, which is accompted the best in Shropshire', and that there was 'good stoare of

41. W.A. Leighton (ed.), 'Early chronicles of Shrewsbury, 1372–1603', *Transactions of the Shropshire Archaeological and Historical Society*, 3 (1880), pp. 239–352, at p. 307.
42. Leighton (ed.), 'Chronicles', p. 319.
43. C. Dyer, 'Woodlands and wood-pasture in western England', in Thirsk (ed.), *Rural England*, pp. 108–9.
44. SA 6900/1.
45. R. Gough, *The history of Myddle*, ed. D.G. Hey (Harmondsworth, 1981), pp. 58, 63. The reference for the original is SA 1525/1.
46. Gough, *Myddle*, p. 63.

sheep ... whose wool if washed white and well ordered is not much inferior to the wool of Baschurch and Nesse which beares the name of the best in this County'.[47]

Similarly Garbet's historical account of Wem lordship provides insight into the character of the local rural economy. The market town of Wem had three common fields in the mid-sixteenth century called the 'cross', 'chapel' and 'middle' fields, and the neighbouring townships of Edstaston, Cotton, Horton, Tilley and Aston also had common fields.[48] The wooded character of Wem lordship seems to have changed dramatically in the seventeenth century as whilst the wood at Edstaston was 'still preserved', the timber of Brockhurst (which had survived as a wood until the Civil War) had been felled and the freehold of the land sold; at Lacon the trees which had formed the wood called Shetenhurst had been felled; Cotton Wood had 'scarce a tree left on it', providing common pasture for sheep and other cattle; and Northwood, which before the reign of Henry VIII had been a large wood, had lost its trees and had been converted into good pasture for cattle.[49]

In Shropshire, a lowland woodland or alternatively a pastoral vale region, early enclosure had a less profound impact on the rural economy compared with other Midland counties, as sufficient areas of open heathland, hill and wooded commons remained. These offered livestock grazing, fuel in the form of timber, firewood, bracken, fern and rushes (estovers), peat and turf (turbary), as well as clay and other raw materials for those with legal or customary common rights. One of the defining features of early modern agrarian communities in lowland pastoral Shropshire was the continued availability of commons. It has been suggested that from the Commonwealth period to the late eighteenth century throughout England a developing gulf separated the open-field 'champion' or fielden countries from the pastoral communities in upland, woodland and fenland districts. In these pastoral areas, communities were motivated by a consciousness of common rights and a loyalty to local custom.[50]

Reconciling regional difference

So what does this discussion tell us about farming regions and rural communities in lowland pastoral Shropshire, and to what extent should Thirsk's view be modified? Is it possible to map more accurately the spatial and temporal pattern of farming and early industry as we know more about aspects of economic and social change? Clearly, as with other woodland counties in England, Shropshire experienced an intensification in its farming economy as Thirsk originally showed, with the growth of national markets after 1660. Subsequent work, particularly that of Edwards, has refined the picture of the county's rural economy, highlighting the numerous sub-

47. Gough, *Myddle*, 265.
48. Garbet, *Wem*, pp. 253, 260–1, 282–4, 307–8, 347, 361.
49. Garbet, *Wem*, pp. 260–1, 358, 283, 331–2.
50. A. Wood, *The memory of the people: custom and popular senses of the past in early modern England* (Cambridge, 2013), pp. 41–2.

regions.[51] Despite the problems associated with probate inventories as sources, they continue to provide a quantitative basis for the analysis of farming regions. They indicate in parts of Shropshire the importance of cattle and sheep husbandry, and especially the specialisation in dairying; the latter originated in the seventeenth century and continues today. Documentary evidence suggests that contemporary commentators like Coningsby, who reported in 1597 that Shropshire was a 'Countrie' consisting wholly of woodland, 'bredd of Oxen and Dairies', was generally representative at that time, corresponding with the evidence of probate inventories.[52]

Clearly there are ways in which we can extend our knowledge of how farming economies changed. Some of the types of land use identified by Thirsk, namely 'mixed farming' and 'pasture farming' ('wood-pasture' and 'open pasture'), changed their characters over time so that one type was converted into another. Shropshire is best defined as a wood-pasture area as in its use of land it contained a mixture of pasture, woods, arable and heaths. During the late medieval and early modern periods it underwent a transition to more open pasture as Thirsk argued.[53] Historians have tended to neglect the woodlands, just as the early modern English state gave so much attention to corn country as it was concerned to keep up the supply of basic foodstuffs. Woodland areas such as Shropshire, along with other 'horn and thorn' regions, need to be studied in order to give a more balanced picture of the agrarian economy of the whole of England.[54]

In defining broad farming regions the variety of small-scale local economies can be obscured. Careful analysis of probate inventories shows the particularities of a single parish, but should the close texture of parochial differences predominate in our analysis, or should we be aggregating the small cases so that they build up a picture of a larger region? Both approaches are valid. We can argue that knowledge of heterogeneity at the level of the manor or parish helps us to reconstruct rural communities and to appreciate the inhabitants' experience of their own farming and landscape. On the other hand, the study of regions allows historians to make sense of a complicated reality. Alternative approaches to regional difference have been developed on the continent, in particular the 'social agrosystems' which take into account a wide and complex range of aspects of the rural economy and society.[55] Nevertheless Thirsk's model of farming regions remains relevant, as it does not focus entirely on agriculture, and takes into account such features as rural industry. Her approach has greatly extended our understanding of the history of rural England.

51. Edwards, *Farming economy*; Edwards, '1540–1750'; Edwards, 'Dairy farming'.
52. Pollard and Blatcher, 'Hayward Townshend's Journals', p. 16.
53. Thirsk, *England's agricultural regions*, p. 42.
54. Thirsk, 'Horn and thorn', pp. 163–82.
55. For example, E. Thoen, 'Social agrosystems' as an economic concept to explain regional differences. An essay taking the former county of Flanders as an example (Middle Ages-19th century)', in van Bavel and Hoppenbrouwers (eds), *Landholding and land transfer*, pp. 47–66.

7

Enclosure, common fields and social relations in early modern Norfolk

NICOLA WHYTE

> In the first two decades of this century, Tudor enclosures received more than
> their share of attention from economic historians. Since then there has been
> no attempt to reconsider the old judgements in the light of new knowledge,
> and by constantly rehearsing old views we are now in danger of over-
> simplifying a complex problem.[1]

With these words, written in 1959, Joan Thirsk set out to reveal the complex history
of enclosure. She cautioned against making 'dogmatic universal assumptions' and
encouraged historians to consider the tangle of motivations informing farmers'
decisions to enclose, or not to enclose, their lands in the past. She impressed upon
her readers the importance of understanding enclosure and economic change, not
as some homogeneous process affecting all people across the country at the same
time, but rather as a consequence of differences in environmental conditions and
inherited farming practices. Thus in heavy clayland regions, for example, farmers
tended to enclose their lands in order to specialise in livestock, often developing
systems of convertible husbandry, sowing crops and grass leys in rotation.[2] In
contrast, farmers on the light lands continued to farm open fields, observing
often very complex systems of sheep–corn husbandry. Sheep were penned in folds
on tathed lands under fallow, their manure being vital to restoring soil fertility.[3]
In Thirsk's words, 'without the golden hoof, the land could not have been kept

---

1. J. Thirsk, *Tudor enclosures* (London, 1959), p. 3.
2. Thirsk, *Tudor enclosures*, p. 16.
3. Tathe refers to lands fertilised by sheep penned in folds. In William Marshall's words 'tathe' is
   a provincial term conveying a compound process, 'we do not mean to convey an idea merely of
   the faeces they [the sheep] leave behind, in this case, but also of the urine, the trampling, and
   perhaps the perspiration and the warmth, communicated to the soil by the practice of folding'.
   W. Marshall, *Rural economy of Norfolk*, 1 (London, 1787), pp. 33–4, quoted in M. Bailey, *A marginal
   economy? East Anglian Breckland in the later middle ages* (Cambridge, 1989), p. 66.

in cultivation'.[4] While she will be well remembered for her work on regional specialisation, she was also open to the complexities and inconsistencies of the decisions farmers made at a local level. Her use of equity court records, among other documents such as diaries and accounts, gave her work a human dimension, bringing to the foreground the differences arising between neighbours over the best and most productive way of using the land. Her work draws the reader into a consideration of farming as being as much about social relations as it was about purely economic motivations. Threaded through Thirsk's writing is an attempt to reconcile the tensions historians face when elucidating historical processes: how to account for change over time and space, while also accommodating the evidence for everyday local practices that seldom fit comfortably within overarching narratives of historical themes and processes.

Just as Thirsk called for historians to test their judgements and assumptions in light of new knowledge, it will be argued here that considerable scope remains for bringing agricultural and landscape history into closer alignment with the recent findings of social history. Whereas enclosure has been generally interpreted by historians as either presenting a grave social problem or as being an essential prerequisite of individualism and capitalism, this chapter will focus on the everyday processes and meanings of making (and unmaking) boundaries in the 'common' fields.[5] Two areas of current thinking on early modern society have influenced the following discussion in particular: first, the rich corpus of literature on the culture of neighbourliness, mutual obligation and cooperation within local societies;[6] and second, the recent work by gender historians on contemporary meanings of privacy.[7] When taken together this literature raises important questions concerning the extent to which farmers were motivated to create enclosed *private* spaces and the extent to which enclosure can be viewed as reflecting the denigration of communal forms of living and progression towards acquisitive individualism and modernity.

Historians and landscape archaeologists have tended (whether implicitly or explicitly) to view enclosure and the attack upon custom and common rights

4. Thirsk, *Tudor enclosures*, p. 19.
5. On the social effects of enclosure see for example, E.P. Thompson, *Customs in common* (London, 1993); J. Neeson, *Commoners; common right, enclosure and social change in England 1700–1820* (Cambridge, 1993); B. Manning, *Village revolts: social protest and popular disturbances in England, 1509–1640* (Oxford, 1988); K. Lindley, *Fenland riots and the English Revolution* (London, 1982); A. Wood, *Riot, rebellion and popular politics in early modern England* (Basingstoke, 2002). On the relationship between enclosure and capitalism see M. Johnson, *An archaeology of capitalism* (Oxford, 1996), pp. 44–69.
6. Especially C. Muldrew, 'From a 'light cloak' to an 'iron cage'; historical changes in the relation between community and individualism', in A. Shepard and P. Withington (eds), *Communities in early modern England* (Manchester, 2000) pp. 156–77; K. Wrightson, *English society 1580–1680* (London, 1982); K. Wrightson, 'Mutualities and obligations: changing social relationships in early modern England', *Proceedings of the British Academy*, 139 (Oxford, 2006), pp. 157–94.
7. L.C. Orlin, *Locating privacy in Tudor London* (Oxford, 2009).

through the lens of modernity. The evidence for disputes at a local level is thus situated within a broader contextual framework of shifting ideas about ownership, the commodification of rights, economic competition and emerging notions of private property. As the old customary landscape was dismantled, carved up and sold off, spatial orientation, movement, places of meaning and significance were dramatically altered. As recent work has shown, it is important that we understand the development of the discourse of improvement in shaping long-term processes of change in the representation of land and property.[8] Blomley argues for the importance of the hedge 'as a device through which new forms of spatial discipline were both materialised and enforced ... The hedge both helped to concretise a new set of controversial discourses around land and property rights, and aimed to prevent new forms of physical movement associated with the communing economy.'[9] Historians would no doubt do well to consider the work of the lowly hedge; but we must also be careful not to overstate the work of the hedge, for other forms of boundary existed to define people's social and economic relationships and their ties to the land.[10] Nor must we assume that older standards based upon neighbourly cooperation were merely swept aside by profit-driven, rational, market-oriented 'enclosing' individuals. Historians have argued that social relations were recast and the meanings of community were ever more tightly defined by the beginning of the seventeenth century. A thick cultural and social wedge was inserted between the 'improving' husbandmen, the better sort of the parish, and the poor.[11] But even as the meanings of community were recast, the threads of cooperation and mutual dependency, and principles of neighbourliness were not eradicated and replaced by atomised individuals, looking after their own interests. Rather terms of commonality and interdependency retained an important and defining role in local social and economic relations among the better sorts of householder.[12]

Johnson makes the pertinent point that enclosure, as with any form of material culture, came to mean different things to people at different times.[13] Thus, as Blomley has also argued, across our period of focus we might track changing

8. A. McRae, *God speed the plough: the representation of agrarian England, 1500–1660* (Cambridge, 1996); P. Warde, 'The idea of improvement, c.1520–1700', in R. Hoyle (ed.), *Custom, improvement and the landscape in early modern Britain* (Farnham, 2011), pp. 127–48; S. Tarlow, *The archaeology of improvement in Britain 1750–1850* (Cambridge, 2007).
9. N. Blomley, 'Making private property: enclosure, common right and the work of hedges', *Rural History*, 18/1 (2007), pp. 1–21.
10. N. Whyte, 'Landscape, memory and custom: parish identities c.1550–1700', *Social History*, 32/2 (2007), pp. 166–86.
11. S. Hindle, 'A sense of place? Becoming and belonging in a rural parish 1550–1650', in A. Shepard and P. Withington (eds), *Communities in early modern England* (Manchester, 2000), pp. 96–114.
12. Hindle, 'A sense of place?'; K. Wrightson, 'The decline of neighbourliness revisited', in N. Jones and D. Woolf (eds), *Local identities in late medieval and early modern England* (Basingstoke, 2007), pp. 19–49; Muldrew, 'From a light cloak'.
13. Johnson, *Archaeology of capitalism.*

ideas of what hedges, fences and ditches came to signify in the landscape, from a communally shared resource to a privately owned and managed boundary.[14] But while these perspectives offer an attempt to devise a cultural and unifying interpretation of enclosure, they assume a linear progression towards modern notions of property, ideals of ownership and desire for privacy. In an attempt to understand enclosure from the perspective of the middling sorts in the sixteenth and seventeenth centuries, their work and decision-making on the ground, a different set of priorities begins to emerge. In relation to the domestic sphere, Orlin has argued that society organised itself around the principle of preventing privacy. In her words, 'privacy inspired an uneasy mixture of desire and distrust'.[15] Most previous studies have dealt with what is for us that most private of spaces, the home; yet these discussions have wider relevance for our consideration of the landscape beyond the dwelling. Just as a locked room might cause suspicion and mistrust, so might a locked gate. If we shift our attention to examine the world beyond the home, there is evidence to suggest that what we might assume to be representative of a desire to create private spaces, and individual detachment from collective obligations and decision-making, was in fact reflective of contemporary understandings of enclosure as being a customary, everyday practice. As a practice rooted in a deep awareness of the mutual obligations between tenants and manor, enclosure came to provide an expression of commonality among tenants.

The remainder of this chapter is concerned with the processes of piecemeal enclosure, that is the gradual, accumulative activity of exchanging and consolidating strips of land in the open fields. In recent years the enclosure of commons, forests and wastes has attracted a great deal of research and debate. Research has revealed the social and political configurations of popular protest against enclosure, and its social ramifications, which led to the impoverishment and displacement of commoners. Much less attention has been paid to elucidating the social processes and consequences of the gradual and unsystematic enclosure of common arable land. In many villages, piecemeal enclosure was apparently carried out without controversy and as a result largely went unrecorded. As such it is often assumed that the conversion of common land to land held in severalty was attained through agreement.[16] But how enclosure out of the common fields was achieved in practice remains to be fully explored. Similarly, given the impetus for enclosure in the period, the fact that large acreages of open-field land survived well into the late eighteenth century, often until the age of parliamentary enclosures, is also worthy of consideration. Using deposition evidence collected by equity court commissioners, it becomes possible to open a window onto the

14. Johnson, *Archaeology of capitalism*; Blomley, 'Making private property'.
15. Orlin, *Locating privacy*.
16. See also B. Frazer, 'Common recollections: resisting enclosure "by agreement" in seventeenth-century England', *International Journal of Historical Archaeology*, 3/2 (1999), pp. 75–99.

day-to-day practices of enclosure. The remainder of this discussion focuses on the arable districts of early modern Norfolk and villages located in the north and east of the region where enclosure was well underway by the sixteenth century.[17]

Medieval and early modern historians have argued that fundamental to the workings of early modern society was the belief in the principles of neighbourliness. The bonds formed between neighbours worked to establish social expectations and hierarchical order within local societies, and were in turn mediated through the landscapes and places in which people dwelled.[18] Material objects, architecture, buildings, parish church interiors, burial places and the everyday landscape – the open fields and commons, routeways and enclosure – all provided a means through which people indexed the terms of their mutual obligations and interdependency by physically marking points of contact. In the village of Hickling, for example, where enclosure in the open fields had been taking place since time immemorial, as was argued at the time, passage across the former open fields was still observed in 1631 but conducted 'not of dutie but in good neighbourhood onely' and, as was claimed, no one had 'anie wayes or right of waies there but by curtesie or good neighbourhood'.[19] For middling households recourse to 'good neighbourhood' was found in prescriptive literature and husbandry manuals.[20] As Muldrew notes, to be at peace, or to use a contemporary term 'quietness', with one's neighbours, was the first safeguard against disputes, and community intervention the most effective method of settling quarrels.[21] Biblical passages from the Old Testament encouraged neighbours to preserve their boundaries in both a physical and spiritual sense. 'Thou shalt not remove thy neighbour's mark, which they of old time have set in thine inheritance' and 'Accursed be he who removeth his neighbour's doles and marks.'[22] The recognition and practical maintenance of field boundaries, routeways and rights of access was in itself embedded in contemporary discourses of neighbourliness, and in turn formed the foundations of profitable farming relations. But ideals of social harmony and good order worked in tension with the demands, inconsistencies and conflicts arising from the negotiation of the physical spaces of manor and parish in everyday life.

17. Identified as the Northern Heathlands and Flegg Loam districts in S. Wade Martins and T. Williamson, *Roots of change: farming and the landscape in East Anglia 1700–1870* (Exeter, 1999).
18. I have recently begun to explore 'dwelling' as a useful concept in early modern landscape research. See N. Whyte, 'Senses of place; senses of time: landscape history from a British perspective', *Landscape Research*, 40 (2015), pp. 925–38.
19. TNA, E134/7Chas1/Mich18.
20. C. Rogers, A. Winchester and M. Pieraccini, *Contested common land: environmental governance past and present* (London, 2010), chapter 2.
21. C. Muldrew, 'The culture of reconciliation: community and the settlement of economic disputes in early modern England', *Historical Journal*, 39 (1996), pp. 915–42.
22. B. Bushaway, *By rite: custom, ceremony and community in England 1700–1880* (London, 1982), p. 82.

Historians have elucidated the boundaries of social relationships, revealing the purposeful nosiness of neighbours, watching and eavesdropping on one another's affairs. The actions of disreputable members of the community and matters of dispute became the 'common talk of the parish'.[23] Research has shown the importance of the neighbourhood in defining the moral order of local societies, and the centrality of neighbourliness in negotiating relationships and calling miscreants to account. While most work has focused on cases of defamation and slander, uncovering rich insights into neighbourly relationships and the self-regulating impetus within local societies, these findings can usefully be applied to our interpretation of the agricultural landscape as a social arena as well as an economic resource.[24] Deponents often related to the court commissioners what they had heard from their neighbours. There was an assumed credibility to the information they offered up, for it was based upon collective knowledge, local memory and the fact that people had seen with their own eyes their neighbours working the land, the observance of jurisdictional rights and boundaries, and transgression of customary laws.[25] When asked for his knowledge of the layout of local rights, and encroachment of the sheep flock belonging to Gimmingham manor on other men's lands, 62-year-old John Wylson, a clerk from Southrepps, told the court:

> he hath *sene* the shepe of Thomas Gryme fermer of Gymyngh[a]m hall feding in the tyme of shack in the felds of Gymyngh[a]m Truch & Southrepps & in no other felds to his knowledge ... *he never sawe* them come farder into Southrepps felde to his remembraunce then to a certeyn waie lyeng on the Est p[ar]te of the p[ar]sonage of Southrepps ... but synce that tyme *he hath sene them goe farder* ... in to Truche felde.[26]

Recourse to the deep past, whether through oral memory or the written word, was important in plebeian attempts to contest change, as Wood has recently shown.[27] As we shall see, the identification of the visible imprint of the past in the landscape was also a vitally important source of evidence in the negotiation

23. B. Capp, *When gossips meet: women, family and the neighbourhood in early modern England* (Oxford, 2003), pp. 269 and 272.

24. L. Gowing, 'Language, power, and the law: women's slander litigation in early modern England', in J. Kermode and G. Walker (eds), *Women, crime and the courts in early modern England* (London, 1994), pp. 26–47; L. Gowing, *Domestic dangers: women, words and sex in early modern London* (Oxford, 1996).

25. Capp, *When gossips meet*; N. Whyte, 'Custodians of memory: women and custom in rural England *c.*1550–1700', *Cultural and Social History*, 8/2 (2011), pp. 153–73.

26. TNA, DL4/14/32, my emphasis.

27. A. Wood, 'The place of custom in plebeian political culture: England 1550–1800', *Social History*, 22 (1997), pp. 46–60; A. Wood, *The memory of the people* (Cambridge, 2013).

of the past in the present.[28] Neighbours, including members of yeoman and gentry households, made assiduous observations of one another's practices. In his deposition, John Boyle, 45-year-old tenant of the manor of Gimmingham, verified that he knew the spatial configuration of customary rights attached to the land, and in particular the extent of shack rights (seasonal grazing rights) over the common fields, for: 'he was borne w[i]thin the sayed towne of Gymyngh[a]m and hathe dwelt all his lyfe tyme there'. Long-term residency was clearly important, but his knowledge and credibility were reinforced through his experiences of the landscape: 'he knoweth to be true for that he hath knowen & sene the same'.[29] Nicholas Bocking of Roughton told the court that the tenants of the lordship of Gimmingham had always enclosed their grounds, copyhold as well as freehold within the town, without contradiction or denial. He recalled when William Baker of Northrepps, to whom he was servant, enclosed 20 acres of land seven years previously: 'And this he knoweth to be trewe for at the inclosing thereof he was p[re]sent & h[e]ard on[e] Alexander whoe sold the aforsaid grownde to his aforsaid M[aste]r & others report the same to be trewe'.[30] Knowing was about remembering, but it was also about seeing and experiencing; it was about being in place and making it one's business to know the geography of rights across the landscape and to defy those who would contravene those rights.

In some villages at least, enclosure was viewed as a necessary intervention in neighbourhood disputes. In Cawston at the turn of the seventeenth century, for example, the inhabitants petitioned Anthony Page, the farmer of the manor of Heydon and Oulton, to enclose a portion of the common heath which apparently lay open to the common of Cawston, the open fields of Heydon and Oulton, and the several or enclosed grounds belonging to Anthony Page. As a consequence of which, 'there doth daylye ryse div[er]se & sundry causes & Actions'.[31] The terms of the proposal speak to a wider sense of social obligation. The tenants demanded that Page make a sufficient ditch and fence with gates needed for people travelling through the 'country'. The tenants also made clear that while they demanded that Page set up the enclosures to prevent further discord within the neighbourhood, he was nevertheless to ensure his newly enclosed grounds would lie open during the time of shack. Between the end of harvest in Cawston until the Annunciation of the Virgin Mary 'the s[ai]d grounds shall allwayes to ley open for the cattell of the inhabitants of Cawston to have there cominage there as in times past they have used'.[32] The tenants 'desired' that their request be enrolled in her majesty's court of the manor of Cawston. In this articulation of farming practice, the terms outlined make clear the sacrifices necessary for both the commoners and Page

28. N.Whyte, Inhabiting the landscape: place, custom and memory (Oxford, 2009).
29. TNA, DL4/14/32.
30. TNA, DL4/14/32.
31. Norfolk Record Office (hereafter NRO), NRS2604.
32. NRO, NRS2604.

for the common good. While the inhabitants had formerly exercised rights for the full year, the proposed changes were deemed beneficial as they would quell the daily antagonisms and disputes arising in an open, unfenced landscape. In Cawston, on this occasion, reciprocity, mutual exchange and good order lay at the heart of the decision to enclose, as did the desire for 'quietness' for the sake of the neighbourhood.

The view that enclosure was a means of mediation to give a village peace does not convey any straightforward correlation between boundary making and the creation of private space. As Williamson has argued, physical barriers were a necessity of open-field farming: livestock needed to be corralled in order to prevent them from trespassing on lands under tillage.[33] This might include setting up temporary folds, as well as more permanent barriers, which might have been viewed as impermeable during the growing season, yet permeable during 'shack time', that is common grazing after harvest.[34] In Cawston, the tenants demanded that provision be made to ensure the continuity of their customary routeways and grazing rights. After harvest the land was thrown open and the commons reinstated once more. William Lockes, aged 76, for example, described how one George Peters of late time enclosed part of Alvington Field, which the complainant now holds in severalty, but in shack time he 'leaveth the gate open & div[er]se gapps in the same wherby the cattell may enter into the same grounds'. Elsewhere, in Gimmingham, John Bacon, a 30-year-old yeoman, gave an account of the negotiation of enclosure within Gimmingham Soke. His oral testimony is worth quoting at length:[35]

> He hath heard that the tenants of the Soke could not enclose any grounds without licence, for he says at a certain time about five years since Peter Reade going a hawking having in his company Mr George Duke Mr Peter Beverley, this examinant and diverse others went down to a covert called Bradfield Carres, and as they went they did see Richard Wortes inclosing a certain piece of ground lying on the East side of Sowthwood, with whom the said Peter found great fault and asked him who gave him licence, to whom the said Wortes said none, and desired him to be content and that he should sustain no loss thereby, to whom the said Peter said that by means of that Inclosure he could not have his foldcourse in shack time upon the said ground, and then the said Wortes answered that all shack time the said ground should be open, with which answer the said Peter Reade was pacified and went his way.[36]

33. T. Williamson, 'Understanding enclosure', *Landscapes*, 1 (2000), pp. 56–79.
34. N. Whyte, 'Contested pasts: custom, conflict and landscape change in West Norfolk, *c*.1550–1650', in R. Hoyle (ed.), *Custom, improvement and landscape* (Farnham, 2011), pp. 101–26.
35. Spelling and punctuation modernised.
36. TNA, DL4/14/55.

Clearly the tenants were required to seek license to enclose from their lord.[37] Manorial jurisdiction and authority was displayed not only in the manor courts but by the presence of the landowner (in other cases it was their bailiff or steward) in the physical landscape itself. Hawking, a manorial right and privilege, provided an opportune time to walk the territory of the manor and observe the farming practices of tenants, and to call to account any wrongdoings. Richard Wortes' reassurances, as remembered by John Bacon, that his new enclosures would be thrown open after harvest during shack time, indicate the complex ways in which people at the time understood processes and meanings of enclosure. The physically bounded spaces were permeable at certain times of the year, outside the growing season. The landscapes under scrutiny were not viewed as being categorically open or enclosed, but rather as an unstable and fluctuating blend of the two.

Judging from the disputes presented before the equity courts, it was common-field grazing rights after harvest and in particular the concept of the foldcourse that were at issue rather than enclosure *per se*. Claimed as a manorial right, the foldcourse was invoked by wealthy landowners of the arable districts of Norfolk, whether they had legitimate claims to such rights or not. This form of sheep–corn husbandry is more usually associated with the Breckland and Good Sands districts further west, where landowners asserted their manorial rights to keep large flocks of sheep on the heaths and open fields, while also restricting their tenants' rights to enclose their lands and to keep sheep.[38] Manorial lords claimed the right to run their sheep flocks across the common fields (including enclosed lands) after harvest, during shack time. In late sixteenth-century Ormsby, for example, 'the lords shepe hadd use of shacke from micha[elma]s until St Andrewe'.[39] As has been found in western Norfolk, attempts were also made to restrict tenants' rights to keep sheep known as the 'cullett flock', and to claim common grazing rights for their cattle, which led over time to the gradual dissolution of commonable grazing rights in the arable fields. In Gimmingham Manor and Soke, for example: 'th[e] inhabitaunts & Ten[a]nts of the Townes of Northrepps, Southrepps & all the other Townes therunto adioynyng w[i]thin the said Soacon ... had at their wills & pleasures used to feade the sev[er]all culletts of shepe of sanse n[u]mber in the comon shack w[i]thin the aforsaid Townes w[i]thout lett or denyall until now of late'.[40] Following a search of old court rolls and records by manorial officers in

37. C. Hoare, *The history of an East Anglian Soke* (Bedford, 1918), pp. 135 and 332.
38. K.J. Allison, 'The sheep-corn husbandry of Norfolk in the sixteenth and seventeenth centuries', *Agricultural History Review*, 5 (1957), pp. 12–30; M. Bailey, 'Sand into gold: the evolution of the fold-course system in West Suffolk, 1200–1600, *Agricultural History Review*, 38 (1990), pp. 40–57; M.R. Postgate, 'Field systems of East Anglia', in A.R.H. Baker and R.A. Butlin (eds), *Studies of field systems in the British Isles* (Cambridge, 1973), pp. 281–324.
39. TNA, E134/29 and 30Eliz/Mich8.
40. TNA, DL4/14/32.

Gimmingham, it was found to be 'lawfull for the shepherd of the mannor w[i]th his dogge to dryve the shepe of the Ten[a]nts owt of the felde to gyve place to the Lords flock'.[41]

Sheep farming in the late sixteenth and early seventeenth century was viewed as a manorial privilege and increasingly claimed by wealthy landowners as their exclusive right. The apparent attempts to instigate foldcourse arrangements, which necessitated, indeed demanded access to other farmer's lands, revived earlier ideas of the social order based upon the manor. Sheep farming was more than an economic consideration therefore, for the exercise of manorial access rights provided a material and visible expression of jurisdictional power over the land, and demonstrated the identity of aspiring, affluent, gentry landowners. Many landowners stood accused of exercising their rights through harassment, intimidation, and constant amercements and fines administered through the manorial courts. Indeed, it seems that manorialism was being purposefully reinvented. In Hickling, in 1632, the complainant insisted that the inhabitants of the said town and their predecessors before them 'could not choose but take knowledge that such a company of sheepe were kept in the said feildes ... w[i]thout denyall'. The tenants and local inhabitants judged the enthusiasm of Martin Calthropp, in his assumed role as lord of Hickling manor, particularly harshly. They alleged that Calthropp sat with the steward of the court, urging that amercements (fines in money) be levied and that lands be forfeited, and accused him of being 'therin farr differing from the Lords of all other Mann[ors] in the county of Norfolk'. They maintained that his designs to implement a foldcourse regime was 'an Innovation or new p[re]tence', and that there was no such right in Hickling.[42] Calthropp was described by Robert Skeet, 55-year-old yeoman, as 'a great man in estate' and the defendant a 'plaine man', and yet as he thought, 'had he been equal to the plaintiff [Calthropp] he would not have given way to anie composition for his Inclosures'.[43] We know that similar concerns preoccupied the tenants of Gimmingham Soke, Cawston, Ormsby and Clippesby, where local inhabitants spoke of their fears of 'the evil beginning of a fold course creeping on'.[44] Often based on rather spurious claims to past precedent, and possibly motivated by the visible achievements of their neighbours a few miles away in the west of the county, the foldcourse took on particular social and cultural meanings among landowners in open-field villages more widely.[45]

41. TNA, DL4/14/32.
42. TNA, E134/7Chas1/Mich18.
43. TNA, E134/7Chas1/Mich18.
44. B. Cornford, 'The enclosure of Clippesby Common and the upstart yeoman', *Bulletin of the Norfolk Research Committee*, 35 (1986), pp. 15–17; see also Ormsby TNA, E134/29&30Eliz/Mich8; and Gimmingham TNA, DL4/14/32.
45. Whyte, 'Contested pasts'.

Enclosure has a long history of course, and none of the activities taking place in the late sixteenth and seventeenth centuries were new.[46] In Hickling, in 1632, 68-year-old fisherman Thomas Goose remembered as a boy the fields lying open and unenclosed. Within the time of his remembrance portions of Eastfield and Westfield, Heath Stubb and Further Stubb had been enclosed.[47] In 1587 Thomas Moulton, 74-year-old husbandman and inhabitant of Ormsby, told the court that he was born and always dwelt there, and could remember in John Clere's time, some 40 years previously, diverse closes were taken in and enclosed in the fields 'in w[hi]ch the lord and his ten[a]nts hadd comon shacke'.[48] Evidently, people held an acute sense of the changes taking place to the physical and social organisation of the open fields within their own lifetimes. Yet many tenants appealed to the deep past, laying claim to the work of their ancestors as a precedent to legitimate their own farming practices. In the case from Hickling, Richard Cubbit, a clerk, confirmed that he was a tenant of the manor as well as being a landowner there. He confirmed that he had not made any new enclosures lying in East Field, but kept the enclosures left to him by his predecessors.[49] In some villages piecemeal enclosure was in fact slowed down, if not halted, by the attempts of landowners and graziers to impose foldcourse arrangements. In the late eighteenth and early nineteenth century parliamentary enclosure commissioners dealt with the remains of open fields, together with a considerable number of 'old enclosures', which clearly had ambiguous legal status. Two centuries earlier the tenants and inhabitants of Gimmingham Manor complained that in the past they had liberty to enclose their freehold and copyhold lands until 'Peter Reade late fearmo[r] denied them so to doe'.[50] Deponents told the court how Reade had told them that 'it did not stand with the custom of the manor that any Tenant ... shold inclose any grownd ... to the prejudice of the foldcourse'.[51] Attempts were made to undo previous agreements made between tenants and manor. When threatened with the reinstatement or reinvention of foldcourse arrangements in Ormsby, deponents reported that should the 100 acres, which had been enclosed by licence of the lord, be laid open again to provide access for the lord's sheep 'it wold be a discommodity to the tenants'.[52]

Court records from the late sixteenth and early seventeenth century reveal that deponents often made a clear distinction between rights pertaining to land

---

46. See also C. Dyer, 'Conflict in the landscape: the enclosure movement in England, 1220–1349', *Landscape History*, 28 (2006), pp. 21–33.
47. TNA, E134/7Chas1/Mich18.
48. TNA, E134/29 and 30Eliz/Mich8.
49. TNA, E134/7Chas1/Mich18.
50. TNA, DL4/24/6; DL4/14/32.
51. TNA, DL4/24/6.
52. TNA, E134/29 and 30Eliz/Mich8.

anciently enclosed and land newly enclosed. In the words of George Wright, 70-year-old yeoman from Hickling: the 'company of sheepe w[hi]ch went over the lands of other men (in right of a foldcourse,) ... did take theire feed in the time of shack over the grounds & lands that hath bene latlye inclosed ... but not uppon Ancient incloses'.[53] Similarly, in the village of Cawston, the manor belonging to the crown claimed grazing rights pertaining to a foldcourse on open-field lands. William Lockes, aged 76 years, described the liberty of shack claimed by the Queen's farmers for their sheep flock in all the unenclosed fields in Cawston except in Alvington Field. Apparently they exercised grazing rights every year from the feast of St Michael the Archangel (29 September) until the Purification of Our Lady (2 February) 'when as & where the lands ar[e] unsowen'. He went on to give an extremely detailed account of the customary status of lands lying in the open fields of Cawston including, for example, Millfield together with a number of enclosures near 'Sparrowes Pit' which lay open and were 'shacked' for as long as he could remember. But the closes lying at Fullingate Hill next to Millfield and a close lying next to Popes Gapp were anciently enclosed and never 'shacked' in his memory. In this case and that from Hickling, a clear distinction was made between newly enclosed lands and anciently enclosed lands, that is lands that had been enclosed since time out of mind. In Cawston, however, and perhaps owing to the complex history of enclosure in the village, the 'ancient enclosures' were taken to be more than 40 years old. Remarkably, the memories and knowledge of local inhabitants in Cawston were apparently mapped in the late sixteenth century, to show the intricate spatial geography of enclosure and customary grazing rights pertaining to the open fields. When examined from the local level, from the 'ground up', any straightforward narrative of enclosure becomes difficult to uphold.

Concluding remarks

Evidently common-field grazing rights, claimed after harvest by both tenants and lords, were not necessarily extinguished on recently enclosed land. Thus, while lands may appear to have been held in severalty, rights and obligations continued to determine common grazing rights or, as was increasingly the case, manorial access to pasture at certain times of the year. The seasonality of access rights, and fluidity of land as enclosed/open, is again worth emphasising as it suggests a very different conceptualisation of the fields by contemporaries, and cautions against assuming all enclosed land to have been considered to be *private*. Blomley has written eloquently about hedges symbolising a kind of organic barbed wire.[54] Yet still in the seventeenth century, as we have seen, the notion of a boundary was not necessarily viewed

---

53. TNA: E134/7Chas1/Mich18.
54. Blomley, 'Making private space'.

as a continuous impenetrable and fixed feature. Such was the complex, overlapping configuration of customary access rights, contemporaries held different and often very subtle ideas of the meaning of boundaries and boundedness. Perhaps somewhat paradoxically it was the ancient enclosures that were deemed to be 'private' spaces, that is land exempted from manorial and common access rights. This classification of enclosed land, between old and new, suggests that for contemporaries enclosure was as much about the past as it was a forward-looking progression towards modernity. We can see therefore the importance of the past in the present, as revealed in ancient surveys and terriers, and fossilised in the physical landscape itself. In open-field Norfolk, at least, enclosure did not signal a break with the past, rather it drew upon past practices and placed the act of setting up fences and planting hedges as a necessary requisite of farming, which was in turn intricately tied to social ideals of good neighbourliness.

The evidence offered in this chapter suggests that there are other ways of understanding the history of enclosure. For many of the changes identified by Blomley, Johnson and others brought members of early modern households closer together to resist the activities of those who would encroach upon their rights. What Johnson sees as the wellspring of modern conceptions of privacy, the atomisation of both domestic space and the agrarian landscape, had complex and multiple manifestations.[55] For many middling sorts of farmers, their decisions and choices were informed by local circumstances, the physical nature of the land they farmed, and the particular configuration of customary rights and obligations. Enclosure and custom were not necessarily mutually exclusive objectives, but could rather work together to provide a framework for reciprocal expectations about how best to farm the land on social as well as economic terms. During shack time, tenants were expected to make gaps in their field boundaries and leave gates open to ensure livestock could roam freely, and thereby demonstrate participation in maintaining the common-field system which drew upon a deeper understanding of how local societies worked as mutually dependent units. The evidence from Norfolk villages suggests that enclosure could work to solidify social relationships while also contesting those who acted outside local norms based upon inherited practices of boundary making in the open fields. Moreover, in investigating, as far as we can, the everyday experiences of enclosure and the meanings of boundaries, the notion that enclosure reflects a common desire among landowners to make private property may turn out not to have been a primary motivation at all. A related issue concerns the extent to which we should observe enclosure as a chronological process of accumulation, especially given that piecemeal enclosure appears to have been fossilised in our period of focus by the encroachment of manorial grazing rights. The archival

55. See also Orlin, *Locating privacy*; A. Flather, *Gender and space in early modern England* (Woodbridge, 2007).

record suggests a rather more uncertain, multi-faceted process motivated by competing social as well as economic priorities. It is undeniably a history of power over the land that we observe, but it is a history that needs to take into account the various ways in which the meanings of 'commons' and 'enclosure' as spatial practices were tested.

PART III

Innovators

8

An early industrial workforce: spinning in the countryside, c.1500–50

CRAIG MULDREW

In her 1961 article 'Industries in the countryside' Joan Thirsk looked at 'industry' as an adjunct to agricultural activity. This conception arose mainly from the location of much of the cloth-making industry, most specifically weaving, in the countryside. Here Thirsk put forward the basics of what would become, ten years later, the key features of the theory proposed by scholars who devised the term proto-industrialisation. In short she argued that cloth working arose in pastoral agricultural districts where farm labour was less intense, land less valuable and manorial institutions weaker. This allowed farms to remain small, and their small farmers to engage in industrial activity to supplement agriculture, as earnings from their land were not large enough to provide surplus income beyond subsistence.[1] This development was in contrast to the industry as it existed in Italian city states such as Florence and in the Low Countries, where the evolution of a cloth-finishing industry required training in more specialist skills that were usually confined to an urban environment.[2]

Thirsk, of course, was also one of the first historians to make use of probate inventories in a systematic way in her study of Lincolnshire farming. By the mid-sixteenth century, from which date inventories start to survive in numbers, weaving was a masculine activity rather than being practised by women, so weavers turned up in the records much more often. As a result Thirsk focused on weaving and, since the inventories of occupational craftsmen such as weavers often had agricultural tools and animals listed, weaving was interpreted as a by-employment to supplement peasant agriculture based on smallholdings.[3]

1. J. Thirsk, 'Industries in the countryside', in F.J. Fisher (ed.), *Essays in the economic and social history of Tudor and Stuart England* (London, 1961), pp. 70–86.
2. J. Munro, 'The symbiosis of towns and textiles: urban institutions and the changing fortunes of cloth manufacturing in the Low Countries and England, 1270–1570', *Journal of Early Modern History*, 3 (1999), pp. 1–74.
3. Thirsk, 'Industries', pp. 80 and 85.

But in terms of employment, cloth making required many more spinners than weavers, or any other related occupation. In the middle ages woollen cloths with various names were produced, almost all of which involved fulling. Fulling was a process using a combination of water, soap, fullers earth and urine, together with pressure and heat in order to force the short wool fibres of the weft to shrink and lock together to form felted cloth in which the pattern of the weave was invisible. The most famous fulled cloth was the broadcloth, which was a very heavy, thick and well-wearing cloth. A Kentish broadcloth for instance was 1¾ yards wide and 28 yards long and weighed 90 lbs. Also popular was the kersey, a smaller lighter-fulled cloth 18 yards long and a yard and a nail (2½ inches) in width. This was in contrast to much cheaper home-produced cloth, woven with a looser weave, or the smaller production of worsted, named after a village north of Norwich, in which fine strong yarn was woven into thinner, strong, unfulled cloth. Various estimates indicate that about eight spinners and carders were needed to produce enough yarn for every weaver, as well as 15 sorters, winders and finishers.

Here, I wish to suggest that weaving was not so much a by-employment of farmers, but rather an industry that had already moved to the countryside owing to the invention of the fulling mill, and had expanded by organising the employment of the wives and daughters of poor smallholders and labourers, who probably had already learned spinning for home production. As the industry developed, it could only do so with access to the labour needed for spinning, and the pattern in England was to continue to employ countrywomen and children, while organising the finishing increasingly in towns. In a later article on the development of stocking knitting as a female occupation, Thirsk not only focused on the relationship with agriculture but now placed much more emphasis on the transfer of local skills in home production into market-oriented production.[4] It seems likely that this same process was important, for spinning as a skill played a vital role in the way the cloth industry developed in the early sixteenth century. As John Oldland has recently demonstrated, the great rise in the exports of English broadcloths from c.1500 to c.1550 were of a significantly better quality than previous exported cloth, and required more better-spun warp yarn.

Eleanora Carus-Wilson famously argued for what she termed an 'industrial revolution of the thirteenth century' with the spread of water-powered fulling mills.[5] A set of water-powered hammers reduced what had taken two to three men five days of trampling in a vat to a few hours.[6] Although the case for an 'industrial revolution' was heavily criticised, as Munro has argued, it provided a

---

4. J. Thirsk, 'The fantastical folly of fashion: the English stocking knitting industry, 1500–1700', in N.B. Harte and K.G. Ponting (eds), *Textile history and economic history: essays in honour of Miss Julia de Lacy Mann* (Manchester, 1973), pp. 52–3.

5. E.M. Carus-Wilson, 'An industrial revolution of the thirteenth century', *Economic History Review*, 11 (1941), pp. 39–60.

6. Munro, 'Symbiosis', pp. 14ff.

very compelling argument as to why the English broadcloth industry developed in certain areas of the country where gravity and running water made fulling mills cheaper to construct.[7] Many of these mills were installed before 1400 by manorial lords who charged for their use, and, initially at least, must have been used for producing broadcloth for home consumption, as exports did not start to rise until the late fourteenth century. This implies there must have been individuals organising the collection, fulling and finishing of this cloth. In Langdon's sample of manors, the number of fulling mills rose by 50 per cent after 1360, and then by another 75 per cent between 1490 and 1540, which roughly matches the pattern of figures for exports.[8] Both Carus-Wilson and Munro also argued that rural mechanisation in the thirteenth century meant that, in contrast to the cloth industry of Flanders, in England the industry moved out of towns such as Oxford, York and Lincoln into the countryside, as evidenced by the disappearance of weavers' guilds in towns.[9] In 1515 in London, for instance, the Weaver's Company was listed 42nd out of 48 in an order of precedence established by the then Court of Aldermen.[10]

We have very good figures on exports of broadcloth which would have been produced industrially to meet the specific quality required by the Merchant Adventurers and other exporters. For much of the fifteenth century, exports remained below 40,000 cloths a year, apart from the 1440s, but after 1479 rose to between 40,000 and 60,000 per year until the end of the century when a sudden rise to over 80,000 cloths occurred. Subsequent years saw a continuous sustained rise to an average of about 130,000 cloths per annum in the period 1547–53.[11] In contrast, exports of raw wool followed an opposite trend, continuing their downward slide to an average of less than 3,000–4,000 sacks a year by the mid-sixteenth century. This long-sustained three-fold rise in one particular sort of manufactured export commodity could not have been possible without at least an equivalent transformative expansion of industrial cloth production.

There is also much evidence that by the early sixteenth century the cloth industry was already well developed in specialised cloth-working districts, including the south-west, the Kentish weald, the Stour valley, the area around

7.   Munro, 'Symbiosis', pp. 37ff.
8.   J. Langdon, *Mills in the medieval economy, England 1300–1540* (Oxford, 2004), p. 42; E.M. Carus-Wilson and Olive Coleman, *England's export trade, 1275–1547* (Oxford, 1963), pp. 138–9.
9.   Carus-Wilson, 'Industrial revolution', pp. 55–9; E.M. Carus Wilson, 'Evidences of industrial growth on some fifteenth-century manors', *Economic History Review*, 2nd series, 12 (1959), pp. 190–205.
10.   <http://www.liverycompanies.info/a-z-list-of-companies/livery-companies/companies-by-precedence.pdf>.
11.   Carus-Wilson and Coleman, *Export trade*, pp. 138–9.

Norwich and the smaller, but still significant industry in Lancashire.[12] Zell's excellent study of the Kentish Weald has identified from probate inventories at least 47 clothiers by the 1560s who were organising the purchase, cleaning, dyeing, spinning and weaving of wool for broadcloths.[13] He has estimated that simply to spin the yarn for Kent's cloth output of c.12,000 cloths a year would have required 3,000 full-time spinners working 300 days a year. But since most spinning would have been done part-time by married women and their children, this figure would probably be closer to 9,000–10,000.[14] The military survey of Babergh Hundred in Suffolk from 1522 tells us about the scale of the industry in a major producing area. It included Lavenham and the Stour valley and was home to at least 119 clothmakers. They were, by quite some measure, the occupational group rated to possess the most valuable movables. Fifty-three of these clothmakers were listed as being worth over £20 in goods. Only husbandmen and yeomen had comparable goods, presumably in livestock. Also, 26 had goods worth over £40, and together with five wealthy weavers and a dyer they possessed £9,793 worth of goods, or 43 per cent of all the assessed wealth in the Hundred. There were also 27 fullers in the Hundred. Clearly this was a very profitable industrial economy which would have employed many spinners.[15]

In addition, all of the population of Britain would have been wearing some form of spun and woven or knitted cloth fabric, and by the fifteenth century the standard clothing of hempen, or imported linen undergarments, worn together with stockings, hose and tunics or doublets for men and skirts or gowns for women, together with cloaks, mantles or jackets for greater protection from the weather was established. But how much was produced at home, and how much was purchased from drapers or mercers? As late as the seventeenth century, advice was still being given on home production. In *The complete English housewife* (1664) Gervase Markham provided a description of what was entailed if a housewife was to prepare the sheared fleece from scratch for the spinning of yarn for the old draperies. The first step was to use a pair of wool shears to cut away any coarse locks, pitch, brands or other foreign material. This coarse wool could be used to fill coverlets, and the good wool then had to be cleaned by washing it in soap and water to remove its natural oils. The housewife then had to divide the

12. E. Kerridge, *Textile manufactures in early modern England* (Manchester, 1985), pp. 1–25; N. Lowe, *The Lancashire textile industry in the sixteenth century* (Manchester, 1972), pp. 20–5; G.D. Ramsey, *The Wiltshire woollen industry in the sixteenth and seventeenth centuries* (Oxford, 1943), pp. 1–49.

13. M. Zell, *Industry in the countryside: Wealden society in the sixteenth century* (Cambridge, 1994), chapters 6–7.

14. Zell, *Industry*, pp. 166–7; C. Muldrew, '"Th'ancient Distaff" and "Whirling Spindle": measuring the contribution of spinning to household earnings and the national economy in England, 1550–1770', *Economic History Review*, 65 (2012), p. 507.

15. J. Pound (ed.), *The military survey of 1522 for Babergh Hundred*, Suffolk Record Society, 28 (1986), pp. 132–7.

wool according to its length and quality and separate it out so that it was loose. The length of the wool was referred to as the staple, which could vary from very short curly wool of c.2 inches to fine wool of 5–6 inches in length. White wool and darker shades were separated and put into different bags according to what colour the yarn was intended to be. If the housewife was organising her own production she could dye the wool herself. She then had to re-oil it to prepare it for carding and spinning. Optimally this could be done with either imported olive oil, or increasingly by the late seventeenth century home-grown rape seed oil. The amount of oil needed was actually quite prodigious, with three pounds being required for every ten pounds of wool. To make a variety of different colours of wool the dyed strands now had to be mixed in the proper ratios of colours, which was done by spreading out a sheet on the ground and carefully laying strands of wool on top of one another until a bed of wool had been prepared. This then had to be rolled up into a hard bundle and small pieces pulled out to be carded. It was an exacting business as all knots, however small, had to be removed. Just the right amount of oil then had to be added or the thread might fall apart when spun. This produced wool to be spun on a great wool wheel for woollens. The thread had to be drawn according to the quality of the wool and not the desire of the spinner – that is a fine thread had to be drawn from a fine staple, and a coarse thread from a coarse staple. Wool had to be spun for both warp, which was spun close and twisted for strength, and weft which was less strong, and, if intended to be fulled, was spun loose, hollow and only half twisted. The housewife was then instructed on how to reel her yarn, and he described how she could then take it to the weaver to be woven according to her instructions. No finishing was done apart from a final cleaning of white cloth.[16]

Dyer has estimated that, around 1500, home demand might have been in the order of 3 yards of cloth per 1.25 million adults, or 4 million yards – the equivalent of 160,000 cloths, or double the total of exports at the time.[17] More recently, Oldman has suggested that this is a conservative estimate as it took three yards to produce a tunic, four to make a lined doublet and a yard of kersey to make a pair of hose. In addition to this, children's clothes needed to be supplied as well as bed hangings, cushions, blankets and other household items. He also suggested that in the south of England, at least, much of this cloth would have been industrially, rather than home produced, and estimated that in the period 1541–5 domestic consumption might have been 190,000 cloths.[18] Although there is no way of measuring this, Dyer, using the Babergh Hundred survey as an example, concluded that if all the other known cloth-producing districts had a

16. G. Markham, The English house-wife (London, 1664), pp. 122–9.
17. C. Dyer, An age of transition? Economy and society in England in the later middle ages (Oxford, 2005), pp. 148–50.
18. J. Oldland, 'Wool and cloth production in late medieval and early Tudor England', Economic History Review, 67 (2014), pp. 8–41.

similar number of weavers per population, then at least 200,000 cloths were being produced industrially to meet a combined home and export demand of about 240,000 cloths. Two inventories taken in 1558 for a Southampton woollen draper and cloth merchant, respectively, list hundreds of yards of different colours and types of cloth for sale.[19]

Certainly all fulled broadcloth for both home consumption and export would have been produced industrially and sold on the market, and as this industry increased so too would the need for labour in specialised areas where skilled workers could train others in sorting, scribbling, washing, oiling, spinning, weaving, fulling and tentering. As a result, the link to upland areas in the late fifteenth century might thus be coincidental from an agricultural point of view, and more related to cheaper waterpower.[20] The link between upland and woodland pastoral landscapes and the transition to industry came under quite severe criticism from Coleman, who pointed out that the most successful early modern cloth industry was located in East Anglia, which possessed very advanced arable agriculture. In the West Country, while there was much more upland and wooded terrain, much land was still cultivated as arable. Of course, then both regions de-industrialised.[21] Also the idea that pastoral agriculture uses less labour only makes sense in broad terms if one ignores the labour of dairy production of butter and cheese, done largely by women. The fact that weavers possessed animals and small plots of land probably had more to do with the household economy, to provide work for wives and children when demand was slack. The sharp fluctuations in exports would certainly have led to changes in demand for work from year to year, although home demand was growing throughout this period.[22]

Later sources, which give estimates of the numbers of workers needed to produce different types of cloth, show that the vast preponderance of labour needed was in spinning. A report of 1588 on the Yorkshire woollen industry from Leeds noted that 60 people were employed to make one broadcloth of old drapery of about 86 lbs. This involved 12 people sorting and dressing, 30 spinning and carding, 12 weaving and 6 doing odd jobs. Of the same number making kerseys, 6 sorted, 40 span and carded, 8 wove, and 6 were shearmen. Here it was estimated that the spinners could spin and card 5.6 lbs of wool for broadcloth and 4.2

---

19. E. Roberts and K. Parker (eds), *Southampton probate inventories 1447–1557*, Southampton Record Society, 34 (1992), pp. 119–27.

20. Fulling mills could be built on rivers as well, but were more expensive as the building of mill pools and races was required.

21. D.C. Coleman, 'Proto-industrialisation: a concept too many', *Economic History Review*, 2nd series, 36 (1983), pp. 441–4.

22. S.A.J. Keibek and L. Shaw-Taylor, 'Early modern rural by-employments: a re-examination of the probate inventory evidence', *Agricultural History Review*, 61 (2013), pp. 251ff.

lbs for kerseys per week.[23] A later comparison was made by the wool merchant John Haynes in a pamphlet of 1715, where he claimed that 'The number of Poor employed in the manufacture of one pack (240 lbs) of short [staple] wool into cloth [old draperies]' in one week was:

3	men to sort, dry and mix
5	scribble or stock card it
35	women and girls to card and spin
8	men to weave it
4	men and boys to spool and wind it
8	men and boys to scour, burle, full, shear, rack and press it
63	[total][24]

These estimates are borne out by a rough comparison of the number of labouring households compared to the number of weavers in the survey of Babergh Hundred in 1522, since most spinning was done by the wives and elder daughters of farm labourers.[25] There 562 labourers were rated compared to 112 weavers, almost exactly five times as many.[26]

Bowden has estimated that in the period 1540–7 the annual export of cloth (including some worsted) averaged 124,750 cloths. The latter, on the basis of 4.33 cloths to the sack, would be the equivalent of 28,790 sacks of wool.[27] Converting this into pounds at 364 lbs to the sack would equal 10,479,560 lbs of wool which needed spinning. Using an average of 4.5 lbs of wool spun per week by a married women spinning for 35 weeks a year outside of summer agriculture, this means there could have been work for 66,538 married spinners working 35 weeks a year, just for exports.[28] If we add home consumption of 190,000 cloths and arbitrarily assume that 75 per cent was produced for sale rather than at home, this would add work for about another 76,000 spinners for a total of over 142,000 spinners. At this time there were approximately 875,000 women and girls above the age of 12, so spinning for wages would have required about 16 per cent of women and girls. This is much less labour than would be required after the development of the new draperies, but the increase in cloth exports from 1450 to about 1550 was in the order of 300 per cent. At a household level, if we assume that most children were employed in carding wool rather than spinning, and that there was the equivalent of one spinner

23. R.H. Tawney and E. Power, *Tudor economic documents*, vol. 1 (London, 1963), pp. 216–17.
24. J. Haynes, *Great Britain's glory: or an account of the great numbers of poor employed in the woollen and silk manufactures* (London, 1715), pp. 5–10.
25. Muldrew, 'Th'ancient Distaff', p. 505.
26. Pound, *Military survey*, pp. 132–3.
27. P. Bowden, *The wool trade in Tudor and Stuart England* (London, 1962), pp. 37–8.
28. Muldrew, 'Th'ancient Distaff', pp. 509–10.

per household this would have provided new earnings for about 25 per cent of households in the country.[29]

Unfortunately, there is even less evidence on what and how spinners were paid in the early sixteenth century than there is for later years, which might give us an indication of the skill required to produce industrial as opposed to home produced yarn. But as John Oldland has pointed out, clothiers were increasingly producing higher quality broadcloths of over 1,000 warp thread counts, which required more strong thread, for which higher wages were paid.[30] An official list of wage rates set by the JPs of Wiltshire in 1605 gave rates of spinning from 2d to 6d per pound of wool, depending of the warp count of the cloth, which, given the 'stickiness' of such official rates, might be what they had been much earlier. Certainly the non-official sources that survive from the late sixteenth century indicate much higher rates for fine spinning.[31] One report to the Privy Council from 1578 on a manufactory set up in Hatfield to employ and train spinners was paying the very large sum of 10 groats for a pound, or over 3 shillings, for 'small' 'even' work.[32]

Whatever the rate of earnings supplied to spinners, they were clearly expanding as demand for cloth grew by about 60 per cent in the 50 years after 1490. Population had begun its climb back up from the continued low level, due to the high mortality of the fifteenth century, to reach the level of growth evident in the aggregate parish register data analysed by Wrigley and Schofield from 1541 onward.[33] But still there was surplus land, as the population had only reached 2,800,000 by 1541, and so the number of self-sufficient smallholders would have remained large. It seems logical to assume that rising peasant cash incomes must have predated the long rise in income derived from the sale of agricultural products to a rapidly expanding population, which formed the basis of Tudor commercialisation.[34] Wrightson calculated that in 1590 the demand for commercially produced food by urban and non-agricultural families might have only been in the order of 65 per cent of production.[35] Recently Dyer has put forward an argument for increasing consumption towards the end of the fifteenth century, and this must have been equally marked in the first half of the sixteenth century. Even if a spinner only earned 2d per pound of wool spun, at a rate of

29. Using a population figure of 2,830,459, and a household size of 4.75 in 1541. E.A. Wrigley, R.S. Davies, J.E. Oeppen and R.S. Schofield, *English population history from family reconstitution 1580–1837* (Cambridge, 1997), pp. 614–25.
30. Historical Manuscripts Commission, *Report on manuscripts in various collections*, 1 (London, 1901), p. 168; Oldland, 'Cloth production', pp. 32–3.
31. Kerridge, *Textile manufactures*, pp. 211–12.
32. TNA, SP 12/123 f. 15
33. E.A. Wrigley and R.S. Schofield, *The population history of England 1541–1871* (Cambridge, 1989).
34. C. Muldrew, *The economy of obligation: the culture of credit and social relations in early modern England* (Basingstoke, 1998), pp. 15–36.
35. K. Wrightson, *Earthly necessities: economic lives in early modern Britain* (New Haven, 2000), p. 109.

labour of 4.5lbs a week for 35 weeks, this would amount to 26s a year, and this does not take into consideration whether carding would be paid for as well.

In a recent critical assessment of wages in the fifteenth century, Hatcher has calculated that surplus cash available to smallholders, after paying for food and other basics, as well as rent and other charges, would have been in the order of only 2s to 6s a year between 1440 and 1479.[36] Even for those labourers working for larger tenant farmers, who could earn up to 4d a day without food by the end of the fifteenth century, this would have been a substantial addition to their family income.[37] After 1500, the price of food began to rise, but according to Clark's price data, this was slow before 1540.[38] Seen in this light, such small earnings do not seem so small, and it might be the case that we need to think about the role spinners played, together with the smaller number of sorters, weavers, dyers, shearers and other finishing trades, in the changing economy of early Tudor England.

Although we do not know the cause of the reduction in the recurrence of deadly epidemics by 1500, we do know that the birth rate in the 1540s was 37 per thousand, higher than at any time before the early nineteenth century. As Hinde has noted, this high rate might have been necessary in the mid-fifteenth century simply to keep the population at replacement level if the limited evidence of high mortality was general throughout the population.[39] In this case the reduction in mortality might well have provided the labour needed for the industry's expansion, and in turn the extra family earnings might have supported a higher birth rate, which might have then helped the commercialisation of local agriculture. These are all hypothetical propositions, but it certainly seems likely that some added prosperity earned through the work of women and children, from a fairly large proportion of the peasant population, paid by wealthy clothiers, must have played a role in advancing the resurgent commercialisation of the early sixteenth century.

In this sense, industry in the countryside takes on a more resonant meaning – not as the adjunct to a non-capitalised system of agriculture with excess labour, but as a driving force of change towards the opposite. It is also the first example of the relationship between consumption and industrial innovation, which Thirsk investigated in her later article on the stocking knitting industry in the seventeenth century, and related examples such as linen, rape seed oil and edge tools, which she discussed in relation to the development of a

---

36. J. Hatcher, 'Unreal wages long-run living standards and the 'Golden Age' of the fifteenth century', in B. Dodds and C.D. Liddy (eds), *Commercial activity, markets and entrepreneurs in the Middle Ages: essays in honour of Richard Britnell* (Woodbridge, 2011), pp. 16–20.
37. C. Dyer, 'A golden age rediscovered: labourers' wages in the fifteenth century', in M. Allen and D. Coffman (eds), *Prices, money and wages* (Basingstoke, 2015), pp. 186–9.
38. <http://www.econ.ucdavis.edu/faculty/gclark/data.html>.
39. A. Hinde, *England's population: a history since the Domesday survey* (London, 2003), pp. 57–64.

consumer society in her Ford Lectures.[40] Presumably those women who turned to producing yarn for the market at a time when food was not expensive did so in order either to obtain better quality cloth for their families, or to purchase other consumer goods.[41]

40. See note 4; J. Thirsk, *Economic policy and projects, the development of a consumer society in early modern England* (Oxford, 1978).
41. Dyer, 'Golden age rediscovered', pp. 191–3.

9

The village shop, 1660–1760: innovation and tradition

JON STOBART

In 1681, an anonymous pamphleteer expressed the opinion that:

> now in every country village, where is ... not above ten houses, there is a shopkeeper, and one that never served any apprenticeship to any shopkeeping trade whatsoever. And many of those ... deal in as many substantial commodities as any that live in cities and market towns, and who have no less than a thousand pounds worth of goods in their shops, for which they pay not one farthing of any tax at all ... If the cities and market towns be depopulated for want of trade then what will the country man do to have money for all his Commodities, as his butter, his cheese, his cattel, his wool, his corn and his fruit? ... It is manifest that the people living in cities and market towns consume all these commodities of the farmers and do help them to ready money for the same[1]

For him, village shops were both an established and deeply problematic part of the English rural economy – one that undermined the traditional roles of town and country. Establishing the veracity of such claims is no easy matter. Most research on rural trading has centred on the markets and fairs which formed the principal means of selling the crops and livestock produced from the land. Holderness and Martin have provided a reasonable picture of the growing number of village shops, the latter demonstrating that traders and craftsmen accounted for anything up to half of households in Warwickshire villages by the late eighteenth century.[2] However, we still lack a clear idea of the character and practices of these shops, or even the range or composition of their stock. They

1. N.H., *The compleat tradesman* (London, 1684), p. 26.
2. B.A. Holderness, 'Rural tradesmen 1660–1850: a regional study in Lindsey', *Lincolnshire History and Archaeology*, 7 (1972), pp. 77–81; J. Martin, 'Village traders and the emergence of a proletariat in south Warwickshire, 1750–1851', *Agricultural History Review*, 32 (1984), pp. 179–88.

Table 9.1 *Rural retailers in Cheshire, 1660–1760.*

	1660–93	1694–1726	1727–60	total
mercers and drapers	4	8	9	21
grocers	1	5	9	15
ironmongers and shopkeepers	6	3	7	16
chapmen, merchants and chandlers	23	20	23	66
butchers and cheese factors	15	23	36	74
physicians, surgeons, barbers and attorneys	7	12	14	33
total	56	71	98	225

Source: probate records proved at Chester 1660–1760: wills, inventories and administration bonds in which the occupation of the deceased is given.

were overlooked by Joan Thirsk in her pioneering analysis of changing supply and demand in the early modern period, falling down the gaps between the urban retailer and the hawker with his pack.[3] Writing a decade later, Shammas argued that the so-called new groceries, introduced to England in the middle decades of the seventeenth century, were crucial in allowing small retailers to build sales and generate more rapid and reliable turnover; but her 'country retailers' were, in reality, small-town shopkeepers.[4] Much of the rest of the burgeoning literature on seventeenth- and especially eighteenth-century retailing centres on the bright lights of London or the somewhat less dazzling, but still well-lit shops of provincial towns. In contrast, the village shop remains obscure. Successively lambasted for stealing the trade of tax-paying urban tradesmen and sucking the poor into debt and dependency, or lamented as a vanishing symbol of an idealised rural society, its doors have remained largely closed to retail and rural historians alike.[5] This ignorance is all the more remarkable given the breadth and depth of changes in consumption during this period; changes which historians from Joan Thirsk to Lorna Weatherill have strongly associated with processes of production and especially supply.[6] If access to goods was so important in determining consumption practices, then we surely need to know much more about the points of supply, both in town and country. This would tell us not just more about rural

3. J. Thirsk, *Economic policy and projects: the development of a consumer society in early modern England* (Oxford, 1978), especially pp. 122–3.
4. C. Shammas, *The pre-industrial consumer in England and America* (Oxford, 1990), pp. 226–9.
5. For analysis of changing perceptions of the village shop, see L. Bailey, 'The village shop and rural life in Victorian England: cultural representations and lived experience', PhD thesis (Northampton, 2015).
6. Thirsk, *Economic policy and projects*, pp. 106–32; L. Weatherill, *Consumer behaviour and material culture in Britain, 1600–1760* (London, 1988), especially pp. 43–69.

shopping and rural consumption would also shed light on the broader nature of rural–urban relationships in the early modern period.

Filling this lacuna is a major task and well beyond the scope of this paper. However, by drawing on a study of village shops in Cheshire between 1660 and 1760, I want to begin by exploring the distribution, form and character of village shops, and then to assess the extent to which we might view them as an innovation within the rural economy. In particular, four key questions will be briefly addressed: first, what was the geography of rural retailing and how did this relate to the distribution of population?; second, what types and mix of goods were available, and in particular were novel and exotic goods offered for sale?; third, what were the ways in which the shopkeeper engaged with their customers, and, finally, what place did the shop and shopkeeper occupy in the rural community – were they bastions of rural society or outposts of urban economy?

Village shops: growth, distribution and stock

Evidence from probate records, whilst spread somewhat thinly, can be used to trace the growth and distribution of rural retailing in early modern Cheshire. The data clearly show both a growing number and widening distribution of rural shops and services over three periods of 33 years between 1660 and 1760 (Table 9.1). Taking a broad definition of rural retailing, to include those providing services such as physicians and barbers, numbers nearly doubled during this hundred-year period. More narrowly defined as mercers, drapers, ironmongers, grocers and shopkeepers (that is, those retailers most likely to be selling novel or imported items), numbers rose even more sharply: from 11 to 16 to 25. Such growth is all the more striking when compared with stability in the number of urban retailers falling into these categories (from 84 to 93 to 92 in the same 33-year periods). Although these figures undoubtedly mask a shift in urban retailing to more overtly specialist occupations (including hardwareman, earthenware dealer and tobacconist), the clear implication is that growing rural demand was being met, at least in part, by expanding rural provision.

As might be expected, the distribution of rural retailing was far from uniform. Early expansion had focused provision in the centre and east of the county, where chapmen were especially numerous and where the concentrations of rural craftsmen, such as tailors and shoemakers, were also greatest.[7] By the early eighteenth century, coverage had become far more even – a process which continued into mid-century – although the Wirral remained relatively poorly served. Again, if we focus on what we might term 'specialist' retailers, then a relatively even distribution is evident, the 47 shopkeepers being spread across 29

---

7.   J. Stobart, 'The economic and social worlds of rural craftsmen-retailers in eighteenth-century Cheshire', *Agricultural History Review*, 52 (2004), pp. 145–6.

villages, from Northenden Etchells near Stockport to Upton on the Wirral. The obvious explanation for this growing and spreading provision comes in terms of increased demand, fuelled through population growth and, as de Vries argues in his industrious revolution thesis, by increasing market-orientation of consumer demand.[8] However, the relationship was by no means straightforward: between the late seventeenth and mid-eighteenth centuries, the number of retailers grew by nearly three-quarters whereas population growth was probably nearer one-third. Moreover, whilst population grew most rapidly in the industrialising parishes in the north-east of the county, retail provision appears to have weakened there, at least in relative terms. This may reflect the nature of demand: butchers, as well as tailors and shoemakers, were most numerous and were increasing in number in these areas, serving the demand for a growing and increasingly specialised workforce of rural manufacturers in accordance with de Vries's theory. To judge from retail provision, however, their requirements remained relatively simple, being principally focused on the basic needs for food and clothing. Mercers, grocers and the like were more prevalent in the richer agricultural areas in the centre of the county where rents and probably spending power were higher. Surplus income here appears to have been more closely linked with the growing range of consumer goods highlighted by Thirsk and others.[9]

We need to be careful here, of course. Differences in the level of provision were not pronounced, and it is dangerous to infer demand (and consumption) from the number of retailers. On the one hand, villagers could also travel into local or more distant towns to acquire goods; on the other, there is good evidence that many consumer goods were bought from itinerant hawkers. We know from the diary of Nicholas Blundell that even the gentry bought from such traders, and that they purchased not just mundane goods, but also items such as calicoes and bone-handled knives.[10] Notwithstanding the undoubted importance of these alternative routes of supply and their undoubted under-representation in the probate records, the number and density of rural shops in early modern Cheshire is striking. Nowhere was more than five miles or so from the type of fixed shop which might reasonably be expected to carry a range of consumer items and to some extent open up a world of goods to rural consumers. Moreover, they were not restricted to larger villages or parish centres. The latter accounted for about three-fifths of village shops, with substantial settlements such as Bunbury, Tarporley and Great Neston each having several retailers who, to judge from the dates of their deaths,

---

8. J. de Vries, *The industrious revolution: consumer behaviour and the household economy, 1650 to the present* (Cambridge, 2008), pp. 122–86.

9. Thirsk, *Economic policy and projects*; Weatherill, *Consumer behaviour*; W. Smith, *Consumption and the making of respectability, 1600–1800* (London, 2002); M. Overton et al., *Production and consumption in English households, 1600–1750* (London, 2004).

10. See, for example, F. Tyrer (ed.), 'The Great Diurnal of Nicholas Blundell of Little Crosby, Lancashire', *Record Society of Lancashire and Cheshire*, 114 (1972), 2 March 1726.

were all trading at the same time. These were places not much smaller than some towns: Tarporley had a population of about 300 in the later seventeenth century, compared with 360 in the town of Frodsham and 500 in Malpas. However, there were also retailers in some surprisingly small villages: Mary Eaven of Newhall (d.1681), John Robinson of Oxton (d.1715) and John Starkey of Cogshall (d.1741) all kept shops in places comprising just a handful of houses and perhaps 100 people. They must surely have drawn customers from neighbouring settlements in order to make their businesses viable, suggesting that, not only were consumer goods locally available by the early eighteenth century, but also that village shops served a population beyond their immediate environs.

As noted above, rising rural demand was linked with a growing ability and inclination to spend on an expanding range of necessary and not-so-necessary items. Even a cursory glance through the probate inventories of rural dwellers reveals the widespread ownership of novel items by the early decades of the eighteenth century. The tailor, Humphrey Walmsley (d.1730), was typical of many respectable village craftsmen. Alongside a range of traditional items, he had an oval table, a looking glass, whiteware and a mustard pot and cruet in his houseplace; a further looking glass in his parlour (used as a bed chamber), and another looking glass, plus four pictures, two window curtains and a range of table linen in an upstairs room.[11] These are exactly the kinds of things that Weatherill marks as becoming increasingly common in rural as well as urban homes, but the frequent and easy assumption is that these consumer goods were accessed via towns. Of course, urban shops were an important source for such goods, numerous studies revealing the cornucopia and sophistication of these as sites of consumption.[12] However, a close reading of the contents of rural retailers' inventories reveals that a wide range of consumer items was also available from village shops.

From his shop in Great Budworth, the mercer Thomas Johnson (d.1686) sold kersey, serge, druggit, linsey, shag, camlet, calico, Scotch cloth, Irish linen, flannel and silk. He also had buttons, tapes, thread and stockings; sealing wax, gunpowder, shot, soap and starch; grammars, primers and psalters; a range of spices and seeds; dried fruits, rice and two types of sugar. Similarly, the Tarporley ironmonger Ralph Edge (d.1683) had 15 types of cloth; haberdashery, woollen caps, gloves and stockings; thimbles, pin cushions, tobacco boxes, ink horns, manacles and spectacles; ironware, including pins, knives, knitting needles and curtain rings; primers, psalters, testaments and bibles; shot, candles and soap, turpentine and oil; dried fruit, seed and spices; tobacco and tobacco pipes.[13] These shops must have been like Aladdin's cave: one can imagine the shelves

11. Cheshire Archives and Local Studies (CALS), WS1730, Humphrey Walmsley.
12. For good overviews, see N. Cox, *The complete tradesman: a study of retailing, 1550–1820* (Aldershot, 2000); I. Mitchell, *Tradition and innovation in English retailing, 1700–1850* (Farnham, 2014).
13. CALS, WS1686, Thomas Johnson; WS1683, Ralph Edge.

recorded in Johnson's shop groaning under dozens of bolts of cloth, or Edge's counters and display boards draped with cloth, ribbon or trinkets. From our twenty-first-century perspective, it is easy to forget the impact that such an array of goods must have had on the men and women who patronised these shops. They gave a glimpse of luxury, a taste of the exotic and a feel for some of the finer things in life.

Three things are particularly striking about these shops. First is the immense range of goods available to rural consumers on their doorstep, not just in nearby towns. Silks, spices and calicoes from the orient, tobacco and sugar from the West Indies, dried fruit from the Mediterranean, books from London, metalwares from the west Midlands and cloth from across the country. It is difficult to gauge the impact that the ready availability of such goods might have had on consumption, but village shops, as well as their urban counterparts, had considerable potential in promoting new consumption practices in the countryside. Certainly, we should not overlook the importance of familiarity and convenience in structuring demand. Second is the lack of specialisation amongst rural shopkeepers. This might be seen as an inevitable consequence of the comparatively small number of potential customers on which they might draw. Johnson, for example, could not rely solely on infrequent sales of cloth, but had to supplement his income with more regular sales of groceries. Whilst such arguments are seductive in their economic logic, it is clear that many urban retailers in the early modern period were similarly catholic in the stock which they sold. Zachariah Shelley (d.1728), a mercer from Congleton, had a wide range of cloth, haberdashery and groceries, whilst the inventory of another mercer, Isaac Newton of Northwich (d.1726), itemised drapery ware, mercery ware, haberdashery and millinery, along with a variety of groceries.[14] Conversely, some village tradesmen were surprisingly specialised. The mercer Richard Smith (d.1716) had £88 2s 8d of cloth in his Bunbury shop, including buckram, stuff, shalloon, frieze, camlet, serge, broad cloth, poplin, dimity, druggit, fustian, check and linen. Besides an extensive range of buttons and small quantities of thread and tape, the only other goods available were a handful of ivory combs, 24 pairs of stockings and 5 quires of white paper. Yet he was clearly able to make a living from this relatively specialised stock, supplying over 400 credit customers drawn from the village and surrounding countryside. Third is the sheer quantity of goods stocked by these village shopkeepers. This allowed them to offer a wide range of choice *within* as well as between product types. As we have seen, Richard Smith, Ralph Edge and Thomas Johnson each

14. CALS, WS1728, Zachariah Shelley; WS1726, Isaac Newton. The actual stock held by urban shops is a surprisingly neglected area. The seminal case study remains T. Willan, *An eighteenth-century shopkeeper: Abram Dent of Kirby Stephen* (Manchester, 1970). For analysis of the changing stock of grocers, see J. Stobart, *Sugar and spice: grocers and groceries in provincial England, 1650–1830* (Oxford, 2013), pp. 41–64.

offered around a dozen different types of cloth, as did Thomas Kent (d.1752), a mercer from Holmes Chapel.[15] There was also often choice in colour and pattern, as well as type of cloth: grey, black, white, blue, green and red woollens, stripes and checks, and printed calicoes were all available from these village shops. Choice was not restricted to cloth: Edge stocked five different types of cap, four sorts of pepper and four grades of tobacco.

What is missing from these lists of stock, however, are the new groceries which Shammas sees as underpinning an expansion in retailing, especially beyond the principal urban streets. Tobacco is found and so too is sugar; but tea, coffee and chocolate are missing. Does this suggest a lack of dynamism amongst village shopkeepers; an unwillingness to stock new types of consumer items? Or is it a reflection of the limited market for these goods amongst villagers in the early and middle decades of the eighteenth century? Inventory evidence is equivocal. Some rural households had the utensils to prepare and serve these drinks: Roger Heald, a chapman from Poynton (d.1719), for instance, owned a copper tea kettle and a tea table, and John Ward (d.1715), the rector of Tarporley, had a copper coffee pot, half a dozen silver tea spoons, various pieces of chinaware and no fewer than four tea tables.[16] However, many other households were apparently without even a kettle. This would not preclude the consumption of hot drinks, but it does suggest that they were not yet an established part of the diet or material culture of most villagers. Supply might thus have been suppressed by limited demand. Indeed, a more general survey indicates that it was not until the mid-eighteenth century that tea, coffee and chocolate became mainstays of the grocer's stock.[17] By the 1770s, however, Samuel Finney noted that the industrial workers around Wilmslow were spending much of their disposable income on tea, coffee and sugar (as well as printed cottons, silk waistcoats and laced caps), which they acquired from the retailers in the neighbourhood; people such as William Wood, most of whose customers bought tea on a regular basis.[18]

It seems, then, that the so-called new groceries were not a central part of the rural shopkeeper's business during much of this period. They relied more on traditional lines and, indeed, traditional modes of selling. Along with their urban counterparts, they invested in a growing range of counters, shelves and nests of drawers which, by the second quarter of the eighteenth century, formed the standard shop fitments with the counter well-established as the focus for exchange of goods. In this respect, there was little to distinguish rural and urban

15. CALS, WS1716, Richard Smith; WS1752, Thomas Kent.
16. CALS, WS1719 Roger Heald; WS1715 John Ward. See also Weatherill, *Consumer behaviour*, pp. 75–9.
17. Stobart, *Sugar and spice*, p. 52.
18. See T.S. Ashton, *An economic history of England: the 18th century* (London, 1955), pp. 214–16; Stobart, *Sugar and spice*, p. 202.

shops, although the scale and quality of fittings was often greater in towns.[19] Selling techniques also had much in common. There was undoubtedly a mix of cash and credit transactions, the latter leaving a much fuller record in the shape of account books which show both the large number of credit customers and the varied arrangements made to manage credit. In spite of the growing rhetoric condemning village shopkeepers for ensnaring the rural poor in a mounting spiral of debt,[20] the evidence suggests that rural as well as urban shopkeepers attempted to match credit arrangements to the customer's ability to pay and to their history of repayment. The practices of William Wood, who had a small shop in Didsbury from which he sold a range of goods, mostly groceries, provide a good example here.[21] Most of his customers were allowed to build up a certain level of debt in the account book, so long as they made regular payments to service or clear their debt. If customers failed to service their debts, Wood appears to have limited their credit. The account run by James Cash illustrates these points clearly enough. He had accumulated a debt of £3 2s 1½d when Wood drew up his account on 12 February 1787. He paid £1 1s of this and continued to buy on credit over the next month, purchasing over £1 worth of goods and raising his total bill to £3 4s 10½d by 13 March. No payment was made against this bill, and for the next two months spending was limited to a total of just 12s 1¼d – about one quarter of the previous level. On 15 May, he paid £2 12s 6d and from June returned to the earlier pattern of spending and payments.[22] Yet these 'modern' practices of credit management were tempered by tradition. Wood also accepted payments in kind, with some customers paying off part of their accounts by spreading molehills, working in Wood's garden, mowing in his fields or mending shoes. In this, he was not unusual, of course: the Kirby Stephen shopkeeper Abraham Dent accepted similar payments in kind.[23]

Village shops and village life

The transactions recorded in Wood's ledger reflect the frequent and seemingly ad hoc shopping practices of many of his customers. If we examine the frequency with which different goods were purchased, we see flour, bread, treacle, sugar, tea and candles were generally bought in small quantities and on a weekly or even daily basis. Soap and sand were also regular purchases, as were salt and cheese; but they were rather less frequent, appearing in most accounts between two and four times each month. This suggests that Wood's customers were buying goods as and

19. A. Hann and J. Stobart, 'Sites of consumption: the display of goods in provincial shops in eighteenth-century England', *Cultural and Social History*, 2 (2005), pp. 165–87.
20. See Bailey, 'Village shop and rural life', chapter 1.
21. Manchester Central Library, MS F942, Customer Ledger of William Wood of Didsbury, 1786–91.
22. Fuller discussion of these arrangements can be found in Stobart, *Sugar and spice*, pp. 154–5; H.-C. Mui and L. Mui, *Shops and shopkeeping in eighteenth-century England* (London, 1989), pp. 215–17.
23. Willan, *Eighteenth-century shopkeeper*, pp. 24–5.

Table 9.2 *Residence of executors of Cheshire rural retailers, 1660–1760 (percentages).*

	same village		neighbouring village		town		other		unknown		total
	kin	other	kin	other	kin	other	kin	other	kin	other	
	n=134	n=47	n=31	n=59	n=21	n=69	n=2	n=7	n=207	n=208	
mercers and drapers	30.2	20.9	4.7	23.3	4.7	14.0	0.0	0.0	2.3	0.0	100
grocers and cheese factors	27.5	10.1	2.9	20.3	7.2	27.5	0.0	1.4	1.4	1.4	100
chapmen and merchants	29.9	7.7	6.8	9.4	6.8	17.1	0.9	5.1	8.5	7.7	100
professionals	24.5	5.7	13.2	7.5	5.7	26.4	1.9	0.0	5.7	9.4	100
chandlers and ironmongers	54.2	8.3	16.7	8.3	4.2	4.2	0.0	0.0	0.0	4.2	100
shopkeepers	16.7	16.7	22.2	22.2	0.0	11.1	0.0	0.0	0.0	11.1	100
butchers	41.8	15.4	4.4	15.4	2.2	7.7	0.0	0.0	4.4	8.8	100
total	32.3	11.3	7.5	14.2	5.1	16.6	0.5	1.7	4.6	6.3	100

Note: Shopkeepers here are broadly defined (see Table 9.1).

Source: Probate records proved at Chester 1660–1760.

when they needed them. However, the frequency of visits made by some customers suggests that other motivations were also at play. Martha Chase went to Wood's shop on 3 January 1787 and bought one pound of treacle; she returned later that day for currants, cloves and pepper. On the following day she bought treacle, flour and barm; the next day she had a manchet loaf, and the day after a further loaf, tea and sugar. On 7 January, Martha bought sugar, coffee and bread valued at 8d, and two days later she had treacle and sugar for 7d. This frequent, almost chaotic pattern of purchasing was not unusual and reflected the very local nature of the customer base for many village shops. But how do we best understand Martha's behaviour? It was categorically not a reflection of a hand-to-mouth existence; that she was not returning to the shop with this frequency because she could afford only small quantities is manifest from her use of an account with Wood. To an extent, it reflected a particular mind-set that favoured frequent purchasing over storage of goods at home; in all probability, it was also a product of the sociability of the shop. We know from Thomas Turner's diary that his Sussex shop – in reality little more than a room in his cottage – was a place where women in particular gathered to drink tea and pass the time with friends. These were practices which both made Turner's days pass more pleasantly and gave him anxiety as he reflected on time

Table 9.3 Ownership of livestock and crops by Cheshire shopkeepers and butchers, 1660–1760.

	shopkeepers (n=16)		butchers (n=27)	
	number	percentage	number	percentage
cattle	7	43.8	20	74.1
sheep	0	0.0	8	29.6
pigs	2	12.5	14	51.9
poultry	1	6.3	5	18.5
corn and hay	6	37.5	16	59.3
husbandry ware	2	12.5	8	29.6
none	9	56.3	0	0.0

Note: Shopkeepers here are narrowly defined as testators identified as mercers, drapers, ironmongers, grocers and shopkeepers.

Source: Probate records proved at Chester 1660–1760.

idled away.[24] Wood's customers probably used his shop in a similar way, a habit made more enticing perhaps by the fact that he appears to have been running an alehouse from the same or neighbouring premises.

These sociable practices suggest that the village shop lay at the heart of the rural community. They were places of informal gatherings, for gossiping and for passing the time – a picture which chimes with our modern conception of the shop as an integral part of the village and a touchstone of its economic and social well-being. However, it is clear that a growing number of eighteenth- and early nineteenth-century commentators saw it as an unwelcome intrusion: it represented urban values (through the goods being offered for sale and the 'modern' commercial practices deployed) and was an unsightly blot on a picturesque rural scene. Repton, for example, neatly expunged the village shop, along with the beggar, from his 'improved' picture of the rural garden.[25] To what extent can these rival images be reconciled?

I have argued elsewhere that we can use the executors nominated in wills as a proxy for friendship networks.[26] Any simplistic correlation of the two is clearly inappropriate, yet these strong bonds can indicate a set of people with whom the individual testator had particularly close connections. What they show is that, taking my broader definition, village shopkeepers had a predominantly local

24. D. Vaisey (ed.), *The diary of Thomas Turner, 1754–1765* (Oxford, 1984), passim.
25. See N. Cox and K. Dannehl, *Perceptions of retailing in early modern England* (Aldershot, 2007), pp. 29–48.
26. Stobart, 'Economic and social worlds', pp. 153–8.

Table 9.4 Occupations of executors of Cheshire rural retailers, 1660–1760.

| | tailors and shoemakers (n=83) | | shopkeepers (n=49) | |
	number	% of known	number	% of known
agriculture	37	44.0	18	30.5
crafts	33	39.3	6	10.2
retail	7	8.3	20	33.9
gentry	2	2.4	9	15.3
other	5	6.0	6	10.2
unknown	86		50	

Note: Shopkeepers here are narrowly defined as mercers, drapers, ironmongers, grocers and shopkeepers.
Source: Probate records proved at Chester 1660–1760.

social horizon, nearly half of all executors being drawn from the same village as the testator (Table 9.2). This reflected the tendency to appoint immediate family, and especially wives, as executors; but in many ways this serves to underline the essentially local world of many rural shopkeepers. Certainly, these figures stand in marked contrast to those for townsfolk in north-west England as a whole. For these urban people, immediate family accounted for barely one-third of executorial linkages, and contacts were fairly evenly split between other towns and rural areas.[27] However, if village shopkeepers were different from their urban counterparts, there were a number of things that also distinguished them from their rural neighbours. First, around one in five of their executors were townspeople, a figure which easily exceeds the urban connections of rural craftsmen, who had predominantly local executorial links. Moreover, most of these connections were with people unrelated to the deceased shopkeeper, suggesting that the association represented an active social or economic relationship between them. In short, shopkeepers appear to have had much stronger links with towns than did their rural neighbours.

Second, shopkeepers, when narrowly defined, exhibited limited engagement with agriculture. Unsurprisingly, ownership of livestock and/or farming equipment was ubiquitous amongst village butchers: nearly three-quarters had cattle and over half had corn and hay, and pigs (Table 9.3). In a very direct way, this reflected their business and specifically the practice of keeping and often fattening livestock locally before slaughter, butchering and sale, either via a stall at the urban market

27. J. Stobart, 'Social and geographical contexts of property transmission in the eighteenth century', in J. Stobart and A. Owens (eds), *Urban fortunes: property and inheritance in the town, 1700–1900* (Aldershot, 2000), pp. 113–22.

or some kind of shop in the village itself. However, the majority of rural tailors and shoemakers also owned livestock or grew crops, possessions which, on average, accounted for two-fifths of their inventoried wealth.[28] In contrast, well under half the mercers, drapers, grocers and ironmongers owned cattle, and a significantly larger proportion had no livestock at all. Agricultural by-employment was clearly not central to the livelihoods of these established shopkeepers to nearly the same extent as it was for butchers, or tailors and shoemakers; they were, in that sense, more detached from the rural-agricultural economy. Third, and underscoring this limited engagement with agriculture, is the occupational profile of executors (Table 9.4). Both craftsmen and shopkeepers drew heavily on individuals from related trades, a reliance which might reflect both family and friendship bonds, but which also made good sense in terms of engaging people with the knowledge needed to manage affairs post mortem. Where shopkeepers differed was that they named a relatively small number of farmers as executors, who comprised less than one third of executors appointed, and apparently had stronger links to the gentry – the latter perhaps reflecting a higher social standing within the community.

Overall, the evidence of economic activity and social links conveys an impression of village shopkeepers as a distinctive, though no doubt integrated, section of the village community. They were more closely tied with other retailers, often outside the village, than with their farming neighbours. The nature of the relationship with other shopkeepers, especially those in towns, is perhaps clearest on those administration bonds which identify an individual as the principal creditor of the deceased. The creditors of rural shoemakers were mostly yeoman or occasionally gentlemen from the same or neighbouring villages who may have been supplying capital, livestock or leather.[29] With shopkeepers, creditors were generally urban tradesmen who were most likely distributing goods to their rural counterparts, in effect acting as wholesalers. The role of urban tradesmen in the supply of goods to village shops was well established in the early modern period. Newspaper advertisements and trade cards often made mention of special rates for 'country dealers'; whilst diaries such as that of Roger Lowe of Ashton-in-Makerfield detail the supply relationship between the journeyman in the village shop and his master in town (in Lowe's case, Leigh).[30]

Amongst the Cheshire shopkeepers, the Mobberley grocer Joseph Strethill (d.1721) appears to have obtained goods from Liverpool, his administration bond being signed by one Thomas Blease, a tobacconist from that town. Still more telling is the case of Joseph Pemberton of Upton on the Wirral. When he died in

28. Stobart, 'Economic and social worlds', pp. 151–3; J. Stobart, 'Food retailers and rural communities: Cheshire butchers in the long eighteenth century', *Local Population Studies*, 77 (2007), pp. 23–37.

29. Stobart, 'Economic and social worlds', pp. 152–3.

30. See Willan, *Eighteenth-century shopkeeper*; W. Sasche (ed.), *The diary of Roger Lowe of Ashton in Makerfield* (London, 1938).

1717, letters of administration were taken out by two merchants, Peter Faulkner of Liverpool and James Burrows of Chester. Two things are significant here. The first is that both men were identified as creditors, suggesting that Pemberton was drawing goods from at least two different sources. The second is that these men were merchants: Pemberton thus seems to have been sourcing his goods directly, rather than using an urban shopkeeper as an intermediary.[31] Both point to a rather different arrangement from the locked-in dependence that characterised Roger Lowe's relationship with his urban master when running his small shop in rural Lancashire. There was a clear reliance on urban tradesmen for supplies, but also a degree of independence and choice. Indeed, our assumptions about the power relations between urban and rural tradesmen are challenged by the organisation of Edward Massey's business.[32] Massey (d.1661) was a mercer from Great Budworth, who ran two shops: one in his village and one in the nearby town of Northwich. The poor condition of his probate inventory makes systematic analysis impossible, but it seems that the two shops were broadly equal in terms of their stock value (around £70 in each). Whilst the Northwich shop had a narrow range of goods (mostly woollen cloth), the one in Great Budworth contained cloth, haberdashery and a wide range of groceries. It is unlikely that Massey could have run both shops himself, and almost certainly employed an apprentice to look after one of them. Given that he was clearly resident in Great Budworth, it seems probable that he took charge of the village shop, suggesting that he saw this as the more important of the two.

Conclusions

This chapter began with a series of questions. What was the geography of rural retailing? What sorts of goods were available in rural shops? How were goods bought and sold? And to what extent were rural shopkeepers linked to and influenced by their urban counterparts? Definite answers to many of these questions remain elusive, but this paper has, at least, begun to consider the spread, role and importance of the village shop; the extent to which shopkeepers engaged in 'modern' forms of selling, and the relationship between rural and urban retailing in the early modern period. Evidence from probate records points to significant growth in the number and an increasingly even distribution of rural shops. This reflects rural population growth, but also implies, as de Vries argues, that villagers as well as townspeople were ever more reliant on the market for access to a growing range of goods. Moreover, these goods, including imported foodstuffs as well as durable goods produced elsewhere in the country, were available at a very local level: few places were more than an hour or two's walk from a shop which stocked a remarkable range and quantity of goods. And, of

31. CALS, WS1721, Joseph Strethill; WS1717 Joseph Pemberton.
32. CALS, WS1661, Edward Massey.

course, these shops offered the chance to obtain information about consumer goods as well as access to the goods themselves. Village shops were therefore central to the emerging consumer society posited by Thirsk nearly forty years ago and much debated ever since. They offered an important window into the world of goods; but was this an urban world (modern and innovative), or did it remain, as Estabrook argues, essentially rural and traditional?[33] The supply of the goods themselves was mostly organised through urban tradesmen, and there is little to distinguish urban and rural shops in terms of the types of goods they contained or how these were displayed to potential customers. Moreover, village shopkeepers appear to have had stronger social links to towns than did many of their neighbours, suggesting a growing urban impact on retail practices and, ultimately, consumption patterns in the countryside. However, it is difficult to judge the extent to which the social and economic lives of village shopkeepers (or the processes of rural consumption) were really influenced by links to their urban counterparts. The notion of rural and urban as separate spheres is untenable, but this does not mean that the countryside was progressively urbanised through retail and consumption practices. The village shop occupied a liminal position between town and country, yet it was ultimately embedded in the rural community, reliant upon village people for its custom and responsive to their needs and desires.

33. C. Estabrook, *Urbane and rustic England: cultural ties and social spheres in the provinces, 1660–1780* (Manchester, 1998).

PART IV

Consumers

Figure 10.1 Isaac Oliver, detail of *Portrait miniature of Richard Sackville, 3rd Earl Dorset*, 1616
Source: © Victoria and Albert Museum, London, 721-1882.

10

'Galloon, incle and points': fashionable dress and accessories in rural England, 1552–1665

SUSAN NORTH

Among Joan Thirsk's many publications on English rural and social history is the research she contributed to the history of dress. Most specific is 'The fantastic folly of fashion: the English stocking knitting industry, 1500–1700', which provides detailed background on a significant, but little documented craft.[1] Some years later, she made an early and considerable case for the relationship between local production and consumption of the materials and accessories of clothing.[2] Thirsk's focus on by-products and by-employments illustrated the complexity of the clothing trades and the ways in which they interrelated. Dyestuffs such as woad and madder, local wool and linen production, lace-making, starch-making, leather waste products and pin-making were all essential in the act of dressing the English at all levels of non-aristocratic society. Not only did Thirsk shed light on the vast increase in humble, local manufactures – so often overlooked by dress historians, who have tended to focus on aristocratic styles and foreign influence – she was one of the first to explore in detail the concept of 'Fashion for the Masses', long before it became a popular approach in fashion history.

In response to Thirsk's research, this chapter explores the shop contents primarily of mercers and grocers – the 'general stores' – of England to demonstrate that a remarkable variety of fabrics, threads, trimmings, tools and accessories, at a wide range of prices, were available outside the specialised fashion hub of London. The inventories selected represent a broad geographical view of England from Durham to Southampton, Norfolk to Lancashire, as well as a variety of communities: seaports, market towns and villages. These have been

1. J. Thirsk, 'The fantastical folly of fashion: the English stocking knitting industry 1500–1700', in N.B. Harte and K.G. Ponting (eds), *Textile history and economic history: essays in honour of Julia de Lacey Mann* (Manchester, 1972), pp. 50–73.
2. J. Thirsk, *Economic policy and projects: the development of a consumer society in early modern England* (Oxford, 1978).

Figure 10.2 Gilbert Jackson? *Portrait of an Unknown Woman*, 1630s
Source: © Victoria and Albert Museum, London, 565-1882.

extracted from published sources, particularly the volumes of probate inventories published by county and city record societies. Also included are several inventories of chapmen and chapwomen, whose much smaller businesses were nevertheless crucial in the dissemination of goods to rural England.[3] In the absence of genre scenes in the English visual arts that illustrate rural and non-élite dress, another goal of this chapter is to paint a preliminary picture of such clothing using the contents of these inventories. It will also define some of the materials and accessories listed in retailers' inventories and show how they functioned in the making of clothing and their place in the complex ensembles worn by English men and women in the period c.1550–1665. Given the well-documented problems of completeness, accuracy and consistency of presentation that attend the study of English probate inventories, as well as the broad spread of dates and locations, the analysis presented here is general and impressionistic. It is a beginning, on which dress and social historians can build more precise and detailed accounts of production, distribution, consumption and self-adornment.

In style and shape, the dress of non-élite English people mirrored that of the aristocracy. The distinctions between the two, delineating a complex and overlapping social structure, were extremely important and relied primarily on the quality of the materials used in clothing, and the quantity and variety of garments owned.[4] Between 1550 and the 1660s, all men in England wore doublet and hose or breeches as their primary garments (Figure 10.1). Cloaks were the outer garments of the well-to-do, but all men who rode or worked outdoors needed coats, jerkins and/or jackets. Gowns were a form of uniform for men of the professional classes, and worn informally by the well-to-do. Bodies (a bodice) or a waistcoat and petticoat (kirtle) were the informal dress of aristocratic women, and the essential wardrobe of the non-élite (Figure 10.2). Contemporary propriety, along with practicality, dictated that everyone wore a linen shirt or smock underneath, and visible linen neck and wrist accessories. Hats, gloves, stockings and shoes not only provided protection for the extremities, but were also essential in a sartorial etiquette that allowed only the face and hands to be bare.[5] Accessories such as belts and girdles fastened clothing and held tools, weapons and purses. During the period 1550–1660, clothing of the élite and wealthy was made bespoke. The man or woman in need of a new ensemble chose and purchased his/her materials from the mercer or draper, along with the desired trimmings, and took these to his/her tailor, who would cut out and sew up the required garment. The tailor charged for cutting out and sewing up the garment, as well as the thread, linings and reinforcements necessary for its construction.[6] Descriptions of this process

3.   M. Spufford, *The great reclothing of rural England* (London, 1984), chapter 7.
4.   S. North, 'What the Elizabethans wore: evidence from wills and inventories of the middling sort', in T. Cooper (ed.), *Elizabeth I and her people* (London, 2013), pp. 34–41.
5.   S. Vincent, *Dressing the elite: clothes in early modern England* (Oxford, 2003), pp. 47–55.
6.   S. North and J.Tiramani (eds), *Seventeenth-century women's dress patterns*, vol. 1 (London, 2011), pp. 9–11.

Figure 10.3 Woman's embroidered linen smock, 1625–30
Source: © Victoria and Albert Museum, London T.2-1956.

concentrate primarily on the provision of royal and aristocratic dress, and the dominant location for the luxury tailoring and associated trades was London.[7] Dress historians have also established the importance of the second-hand clothing market, with the implication that poorer members of society relied primarily on this source. Published inventories reveal the existence of tailors in small towns and villages, as well as larger regional centres, and their presence, along with all the materials for the bespoke production of clothing, suggest that they were available throughout England, if only for 'local élites'.

The foundation of everyone's clothing was their 'wearing' linen (underwear). A man's linen shirt and a woman's linen smock – similar, although not identical, in style – and the quality of the fabrics from which they were made distinguished one's place in society (Figure 10.3). Royalty and the aristocracy

7.   J. Arnold, *Queen Elizabeth's wardrobe unlock'd* (Leeds, 1988), chapter 8; R. Strong, 'Charles I's clothes for the years 1633 to 1635', *Costume*, 14 (1980), pp. 73–89.

wore the finest linens imported from the Low Countries and Flanders – cambric from Cambrai, lawn from Laon and 'holland', a tradition extending back to at least the fourteenth century.[8] England had its own linen industry, but the fabrics produced could not rival those of the Continent. As Thirsk relates in *Economic policies*, some of the earliest 'projects' involved encouraging the manufacture of English linens.[9] However, English linens did not replace the fine imported linens, but increased and improved the quality and quantity of local products for general consumption.

The inventories illustrate the availability of both imported and local linens. Edward Brat, a Worcester mercer (1552),[10] had over £22 of 'holland' in his stock; the 'lynen clothe' was probably of English manufacture and his 'canvas' imported. The nomenclature of linens (made of both hemp and flax fibres) is notoriously complicated, but English products appear not to have been given local names, appearing instead as variations of the words, 'linen', 'flaxen' or 'hempen'.[11] France was the source of a range of canvases, some of which were very fine. Southampton merchants had huge quantities in their inventories; John Lughting (1564) had 32 varieties of both coarse and fine French canvases, ranging from 3d to 16d per ell. In the inventory of Richard Thompson of Richmond (1572) were two types of canvas, four of linen cloth, and also nettlecloth. Only the 'linen cloth' was a local manufacture; the nettle cloth, made from the baste fibres of nettles, was imported from Scotland.[12]

Despite the best efforts of 'projectors', continental imports retained a significant portion of the linen market. The inventory of Charlbury (Oxfordshire) mercer Thomas Harris (1623) shows the new entries in this competition in the early seventeenth century. In addition to holland, cambric and sackcloth (a French import and not necessarily a coarse product for sacks), he has 'ossenbriges' and 'slease', inexpensive German linens from Osnabrück and Silesia, 'inder lins' from Hamburg, as well as 'calico' – a 'linen' made from cotton fibre – from India via the East India Company.[13] This variety of English, Scottish, French, Dutch, German and Indian fabrics continues to appear in drapers' and mercers' inventories well into the eighteenth century. Inventories of chapmen and women demonstrate that those in rural areas also bought this wide range

8. K. Staniland, 'Richard Whittington and his sales to the Great Wardrobe in the years 1392 to 1394', *Costume*, 44 (2010), pp. 12–19, at p. 14.
9. Thirsk, *Economic policy and projects*, pp. 40 and 73–4.
10. Dates of the inventories shown in brackets in lieu of footnotes; citations for the inventories can be found in the appendix at the end of the chapter.
11. N. Evans, *The East Anglian linen industry: rural industry and local economy, 1500–1850* (Aldershot, 1985), p. 37.
12. P. Baines, *Linen hand spinning and weaving* (London, 1989), p. 184.
13. S. North, 'Dress and hygiene in early modern England: a study of advice and practice', PhD thesis (London, 2012), see chapter 2 for linen definitions.

Figure 10.4 A man's doublet and breeches of twill worsted, 1630s
Source: © Victoria and Albert Museum, London, T.29-1938

of linens as early as the 1580s. William Davis of Winslow (Buckinghamshire, 1588) sold Lancashire cloth along with imported holland, lockram and dowlas; and Richard Trendell of Linge (Norfolk, 1596) offered holland, lawn, cambric and 'white canvas' (one of the finer qualities of hemp fabric). These linens served a sartorial function beyond underwear and accessories. 'Childbed linen' was the clothing and bedding for an infant during the first two years of life. The heavier varieties of linen were also used for outer garments such as doublets, breeches, waistcoats and petticoats for the non-élite classes, as well as linings and reinforcements inside clothing.

The fabrics used for outer garments were also a crucial sartorial division of class. Silk predominated in the wardrobes of the aristocracy and wealthy, with wool the foundation of everyone else's clothing (Figure 10.4). Price and exclusivity, as well as the aesthetic properties of these materials dictated this division. From the mid-sixteenth to the mid-seventeenth century, almost all silk fabrics were imported from Italy. Wool in the form of woollen broadcloth had been England's primary textile industry since the middle ages. The development of new fabrics made of worsted in a variety of weave structures and weights was a key economic project.[14] These were known as the new draperies and appear under a variety of names such as says, bays and frisado in the inventories of drapers and mercers in rural and regional England.[15] Kendal clothier Richard Gurnell (1555) sold the products of the worsted manufacturers for which the town in Westmorland was famous: kersey and twill. James Backhouse of Kirby Lonsdale (Westmorland, 1578) stocked the new draperies – frisado, mockado, baize, camlet – as well as worsted, kersey and the traditional broadcloth. This expansion in the range of wools available prompted an early example of commercial 'branding' as manufacturers strove to label their new fabrics with persuasive or descriptive names; those suggesting durability were particularly popular. Anthony Dennis of Darlington (Co. Durham, 1611) sold 'brackotilloe', 'perpetuan' and 'phillisselloes' along with the more immediately identifiable serge and cotton (a type of worsted). Other varieties of wool fabric available included stammel, russet (a weave as well as a colour), wadmal and Deroy; the names of fabrics such as Peniston, Keighley and Bolton indicate their place of manufacture.

Encouragement of the English manufacture of fustian was one of the four major 'projects' of Edward VI's reign.[16] This fabric was initially a blend of linen warp and a woollen weft, brushed to resemble the more expensive broadcloth, and used for the same purposes in clothing. By the sixteenth century, cotton fibre had replaced wool in the best imported fustians. Milan and Genoa produced the finest

---

14. Thirsk, *Economic policy and projects*, p. 44.
15. N.B. Harte (ed.), *The new draperies in the Low Countries and England, 1300–1800* (Oxford, 1997).
16. Thirsk, *Economic policy and projects*, p. 42.

and Germany a coarser quality.[17] These fabrics appear in inventories as early as 1552; Brat had £7 worth of fustian. When listed as fustian (also known as 'bustian' and 'buffin') such fabric was probably English, whereas 'millaine' was imported from Milan, 'gean', 'jean' and 'jane' from Genoa, 'holmes' and 'homes' from Ulm in Germany. By the early seventeenth century, however, jean and holmes indicated the type of fabric rather than place of manufacture, as illustrated by the reference to 'Dutch Jeanes' in Worcester mercer, Thomas Cowcher's inventory (1643).

While silk remained the preserve of the wealthy and beyond the affordability of most, this expensive, imported fabric can be found in small amounts in mercers' and grocers' inventories throughout the period. Brat's inventory featured 2¾ yards of velvet – the most expensive type of silk. This was not enough to make a doublet or breeches, but would have probably been used for accessories, such as hats, or to trim a wool garment. Even chapmen such as Davis sold velvet and taffeta (tabby) providing small amounts of this exclusive luxury in rural England. Silk blended with wool or linen were popular and cheaper substitutes for pure silk fabrics, for example in the form of 'silk rash' (mixed with wool) and 'Sypers' (cypress, silk/linen). Attempts to raise silkworms in England in order to establish a local industry – another ambitious project – proved unsuccessful, but a more realistic alternative was the importation of silk yarn to be woven in England.[18] By 1665, Lincoln mercer Benjamin Marshall had varieties of silks such as satin, alamode and sarcenet, possibly of English manufacture, as well as imported 'Persian'.

A remarkable variety of colours of wool is described in the inventories of woollen-drapers such as Richard Hawkins (Southampton, 1558) and John Browne (Stratford-upon-Avon, 1586). Some wool fabrics remained undyed and were recorded as sheep's colour (these too came in a range of hues). Certainly, darker shades predominate and these would have been practical for 'workaday' clothing, as well as for the professional classes (clerks, schoolteachers, clergy) – black, friar's gray, iron gray, rat's colour, and puke. Brighter hues were also sold – green, red, purple (including 'violet-in-the-grain' dyed with expensive cochineal) – and the highly impractical white. In addition, the inventories offer a further selection of vividly named shades: horseflesh, maiden hair, deer colour, tawny, amber, primrose, sage, willow, frost-upon-green, sky-colour, milk-and-water, sea-water, watchet, carnation, brick, ash and pheasant's-colour.[19] There were medley, mottled, mingled and changeable shades. References to 'a new coller' in drapers' stocks suggest a steady supply of novel and subtle shades. Even if reserved for 'Sunday best', the variety paints a vivid picture of dress in English provinces.

17. P.A. Sykas, 'Fustians in Englishmen's dress: from cloth to emblem', *Costume*, 43 (2009), pp. 1–18.
18. Thirsk, *Economic policy and projects*, p. 7; E. Kerridge, *Textile manufactures in early modern England* (Manchester, 1985), pp. 141–2.
19. C.W. Cunnington and P. Cunnington, *Handbook of English costume in the sixteenth century* (London, 1954), pp. 214–16 for colour definitions.

Supporting the argument for locally made, bespoke clothing for the better-off members of rural and small-town society is the presence of the tools and other materials needed by tailors and seamstresses. Buckram (coarse linen stiffened with glue) reinforced bodies and doublets; the latter were also stiffened with pasteboard, and whalebone provided more rigid support.[20] These are listed in Cowcher's inventory (1643) as '1 dozen & 10 pere of bellipeecs at 2s 4d all / Collers, bellipecs & buskes 9s all' and Harris (1623) had 7½ lbs of whalebone at 6d per pound-weight in his shop. Thread was an essential sewing material; Bristol shopkeeper Thomas Nelmes (1634) sold several types:

> 1 lb of whited Thrid
> 1 Butt of Black Thrid
> 2 lbs of peecing thrid
> 1 lb of slipp thrid
> 4 lbs & halfe of outnall [Oudenaarde] Thrid

Sewing thread was made of either linen or silk, the latter designated as 'sewing' or 'stitching silk' and sold by weight to distinguish it from woven silk fabrics. Needles and pins were used in the sewing process, the latter also fastened clothing, particularly women's garments, and were numbered in the thousands; the shop of Backhouse carried 'xvj thowsand of pynes'. Both pins and needles were sold by the dozen, the packet, the cloth and the paper.

The tools for a variety of other methods of fastening clothing are found in the inventories. Buttons had been around since the fourteenth century and came in many materials – thread or Dorset (made of linen thread wrapped around a circle of horn), hair (probably horsehair), silk, stone, wire, gimp, 'Quick sylver and brase' and glass, as well as silver and gold (silver-gilt). There were special thread buttons used on the corners of handkerchiefs, 'handcharves buttons', 'long buttens for clockes [cloaks]', 'wastband buttons', and some buttons were sold with matching braided loops. Clothes were traditionally 'laced' together, that is fastened with 'points', a ribbon or length of braid threaded through pairs of eyelet holes in each of the garments to be joined. In the sixteenth century, sleeves were laced into doublets and bodies, doublets were laced to breeches, and bodies to petticoats. The term 'points' refers to the aiglets or metal tips (similar to the plastic end of a modern shoelace) that eased the threading through eyelets. Plain ribbons without aiglets, could be similarly used with the aid of a bodkin (large blunt needle). Points abound by the dozen and the gross in the stocks of mercers, grocers and haberdashers, made of thread (linen, probably braided), silk (also braided) and leather; 'ribbon points' indicate woven ribbons. Such a means of securing garments had the advantage of adding decorative bows to an ensemble.

20. J. Arnold, *Patterns of fashion 3* (London, 1985), see illustrations 184, 329, 300.

Figure 10.5 A woman's linen waistcoat embroidered with crewel thread, 1630s
Source: © Victoria and Albert Museum, London, T.843-1974.

Another form of tied fastening were 'shirt strings' and 'band strings', short lengths of narrow, braided linen used to fasten the collars and cuffs of shirts and smocks, as well as separate linen bands (collars) and cuffs. Metal fastenings such as clasps, hooks and eyes were in use for clothing in the sixteenth century. The 'hokes and eyes' in Brat's inventory may have been for this purpose; the two dozen 'claspes for clocks [cloaks]' in Backhouse's shop certainly were. Harris sold 'Hookes & iues for briches' and Cowcher had '7 [gross] of breech hooks & eis'.

The clothing of the aristocracy was lavishly decorated with embroidery, as well as ribbons and laces (of various structures) of coloured silks and metal threads. The presence of a huge variety of similar embellishments, made of more humble materials, indicates that there must have been a market for them, among the country gentry, professional classes and wealthy yeomanry, at least. Metal embroidery threads occasionally appear in inventories; Brat had 'sowying gold' and the stock of James Willinson, mercer of Knaresborough (Yorkshire, 1558), contained 4 shillings-worth of 'Venis golde'. Cowcher had '2¼ ounces of Venus silver at 4s 10d per ounce' and '4 ounces of Venus gold at 5s 8d'.[21] Cowcher also had '7¾ pounds of cull' silke at 24s per lb', in other words, coloured silk thread for embroidery. Perhaps more within the means of the rural élite was crewel, a

---

21.   Venice was the source of the finest metal embroidery threads; see Arnold, *Queen*, p. 375.

less expensive embroidery thread made of wool, which produced as colourful an effect as silk (Figure 10.5). Cowcher's inventory also listed 'Skeyne Crule 12 pound & quarter at 3s 6d per lb', and Harris had '8 oz of cullerd worsted at 6d per oz'.

A wide variety of laces also appear in inventories. The noun 'lace' was used more broadly in the early modern period than it is now and references in inventories and accounts can refer to three different types: lace as a fastening as described above, needle or bobbin lace, or a woven ribbon. In modern parlance, lace refers to two specific textile structures – needle lace and bobbin lace. The former employs embroidery stitches over threads, and the latter is constructed by twisting and plaiting threads around pins arranged in a pattern.[22] Bobbin lace (made with threads wound on carved wooden bobbins) was also known as 'bone lace' in the early modern period, referring to the use of sheep's wrist, ankle and toe bones for winding the yarn, or fish or splintered chicken bones to mark the patterns.[23] Imported Italian needlelace was far beyond the means of all but royalty and aristocracy and it does not appear in the inventories surveyed. England had its own bobbin lace industry in Buckinghamshire, Bedfordshire, Devon and Northamptonshire, another of the projects outlined by Thirsk, producing very modest versions of the finery edging ruffs in aristocratic portraits.[24] These were narrow borders of simple lace patterns, used to edge linen bands, cuffs, caps, coifs and baby linens. The large amounts and modest prices of these laces suggest that they were purchased by the rural wealthy.

> 'Ribbon silke, pirled lace, bone lace and sowing silke, £3 17s 10d' (Brat)
> 'Bobing lace, 6d per oz' (Backhouse)
> '4½ dozen bobinlace, 5s 3d' (Matthew Markland, Wigan mercer, 1617)
> '42 yardes of bonlase, 4s' (Avis Clarke, Stratford-upon-Avon chapwoman, 1624)
> '1 parcell of bonlace & other trifles at £1 10s' (Thomas Nelmes)
> '4 dozen 8 yards of bobbin lace at 18d per dozen, 7s' (Cowcher)
> 'Bone Lace, £1 6s 8d' (Francis Woodhouse, Chesterfield draper, 1647)

Other cheap versions of bobbin lace were also available. Fine bobbin lace sometimes incorporated very thin strips of parchment in its structure to add colour and texture.[25] More coarsely worked bobbin laces with thicker pieces of parchment were less expensive; Brat stocked 'parchement lace' and Nelmes had one gross of 'pummett lace' at 6s. Lace made with silver and silver-gilt threads embellished aristocratic dress, but, remarkably, these too were available from mercers outside London. Markland had 18 yards of gold and silver lace, valued

22. P. Earnshaw, *A dictionary of lace* ((Aylesbury, 1982), plates 14 and 24a.
23. Earnshaw, *Dictionary*, p. 21.
24. Thirsk, *Economic policy and projects*, pp. 6, 66 and 73–4.
25. S.M. Levey, *Lace: a history* (Leeds, 1983), p. 38; C. Thornton, 'Satin bodice', in S. North and J. Tiramani (eds), *Seventeenth-century women's dress patterns*, 2 (London, 2012), pp. 58, 60 and 70.

Figure 10.6 Silk wedding suit of Sir Edmund Verney, c.1662, Claydon House
Source: Courtesy of the National Trust.

at 9s. Copper plated with silver or gold was a cheaper version of the real thing; Backhouse stocked 'Coper lase gold and sylver, 10d per doz' and 'Coper lase gold, 18d'. The 'white olcamee [alchemy] lace' and 'olcamee oes [sequins]' in Cowcher's inventory were probably lead or brass substitutes for silver and gold. Combining metal with less expensive silk thread was another alternative. Thomas Deakin's Lichfield shop (1660) had '2 grose of silke and silver lace, £2 4s, 3 doz. off silke and silver lace, £1'.

'Lace' in early modern literature can also refer to a narrow woven decoration, what we now call ribbon or braid.[26] Ribbons appear in almost every mercer's or grocer's inventory. Cotton [worsted] ribbon was available, but silk ribbons appear far more frequently in the inventories. In 1643, Cowcher's included 19½ dozen of scarlet and black, 10 dozen and 5 yards of 'shadowed' (chiné) and 15 yards of broad orange silk ribbons. By comparison, Marshall's 1665 inventory lists black ribbon in amounts of 46 yards, 26 yards, 16 yards, 54 yards and 33 yards, as well as coloured ribbons in roughly equivalent amounts. This vast increase in ribbon 'mileage' probably reflects more than just the different sizes of the shops involved. The introduction of the Dutch engine-loom to England in 1610 led to an explosion in the use of ribbon decoration in fashionable clothing.[27] Over 200 metres of coloured silk ribbon decorates the wedding suit made c.1662 for Edmund Verney, now in the National Trust collection at Claydon (Figure 10.6).[28] The plethora of like materials in Marshall's inventory suggest that this new fashion was widely copied by young men outside London.

Many types of more modest woven lace appear in the inventories. One of the most ubiquitous is incle (inkle, yncle, encle, etc.), a ribbon or tape made of linen, used for reinforcing and binding clothing and household textiles, for apron strings and drawstrings for coifs and smocks. It was usually white and a plain weave, but the inventories reveal other varieties – carnation, blue, 'coloured' and checked incle, herringbone and diaper weaves – suggesting decorative uses. References to Welsh and Manchester incle indicate places of manufacture, and it was sold by the dozen, the gross, the piece, the roll and in parcels. Worsted ribbon or tape was usually called 'caddice' or 'caddas'.[29] Galloon was a broad patterned (either in weave or colour) lace, frequently used for livery, made of linen, silk and wool.[30] 'Filleting' was another type of tape of various weaves.[31] Cowcher's inventory listed:

26. K.E. Lacey, 'The production of 'narrow ware' by silkwomen in fourteenth- and fifteenth-century England', *Textile History*, 18 (1987), pp. 187–204.
27. Kerridge, *Textile*, pp. 172–3.
28. L. Edwards, '"Dres't like a may-pole": a study of two suits of c.1660–62', *Costume*, 19 (1985), pp. 75–93.
29. F.M. Montgomery, *Textiles in America 1650–1870* (New York, 1984), p. 183.
30. Montgomery, *Textiles*, p. 245.
31. Montgomery, *Textiles*, p. 238.

8½ peeces of fine white fillet at 15d per piece, 10s
4 peeces more of fine fillett at 18d per piece, 6s
4½ papers of fillett & bind at 3s 2d per piece, £1 10d [sic]

Another narrow ware appearing frequently in the inventories is 'statute lace', so called because its dimensions and properties were dictated by law.[32] Backhouse had one gross as well as one 'paper of statut lace', Dennis had 'statine lace', and Deakin 'six dozen of statue lace'. In Cowcher's inventory, the 'sta: lace' is grouped with other 'crule [crewel] wares', implying that statute lace was made of wool.

Fringe is another form of trimming found in the inventories. It was widely used for horse trappings and often appears in conjunction with such items. For example, Backhouse had 2 pounds of 'sadler fringe', Deakin had '2 crewill rains and fring' and amongst Cowcher's crewel goods were:

6 pere of bridle Reines at 17d per pair
2 pound of Crule freinge at 4s 8d per lb
3 pound & half of Crule freinge at 3s 4d per lb
10 dozen & half of sadle butt' & loops at 6d per dozen

Fringe also adorned gloves and Backhouse stocked 'glover fringe'. Another linen waistcoat (Figure 10.5) in the collection of the Victoria and Albert Museum is a rare example of crewel needlework and it has a wool fringe around the hem, instead of the metal lace that edges the finer silk embroidered garments. Nicholas Elcocke (1620) of Stockport had 1¼ pounds of 'singe [single?] blacke fringe'; Markland sold both wool and silk fringe.

The properly dressed English person of any class required an ensemble of accessories: hats, gloves, belts, stockings and shoes. All but the latter appear abundantly in the inventories of mercers, grocers and haberdashers. Covering the head was essential to good health and the removal of the hat an important sign of respect. Outdoors both men and women wore felt hats; hoods were also appropriate for women. The head was covered indoors as well; men wore 'night caps' (these were not intended for sleeping in) and women wore coifs and crosscloths or forehead clothes. Numerous examples of both survive in museum collections and the elaborately decorated versions worn by the aristocracy are occasionally depicted in portraits (Figures 10.7 and 10.8). Backhouse had an extensive selection of headwear:

32.   The exact nature of 'statute lace' remains undefined. A search for it in *Early English Books Online* revealed that it was probably made of wool (a pun on 'cruel' in W. Dugard, *A humble remonstrance presented to the right worshipfull company of Merchant-Tailors*, 1661), but could contain silk (a rejected bill regarding wool and silk textiles in *Historical collections or, an exact account of the proceedings of the four last parliaments of Q. Elizabeth*, 1680). In the rates listed in *An act for the redemption of captives* (1650) 'statute lace' was charged as an export.

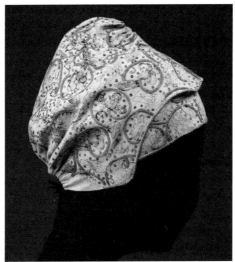

Figure 10.7 A man's embroidered linen
night cap, 1600–30
Source: © Victoria and Albert Museum,
London, 2016-1899.

Figure 10.8 A woman's embroidered linen coif
and forehead cloth, 1600–50
Source: © Victoria and Albert Museum, London,
T.53-1947.

> A taffetye hatt at 6s 8d ...
> 2 felts, 2s 8d ...
> 4 chamlett hats, 12s
> A mockadaw hatt, 3s
> 4 taffetye hats for children, 5s
> 2 sylk hats course, 8s ...
> Felt hats, 3s 4d

The fabric hats, silk, including taffeta, mockado (wool/silk velvet) and camlet, were probably the 'milan bonnet' and caps fashionable in the first half of the sixteenth century and still being worn outside London.[33] Felt hats were the latest style of blocked headwear, made of either rabbit or beaver fur. A 'felt' was a soft, unshaped cone of felt which required further blocking (shaping while damp over a wooden block) to mould it into a fashionable style, and Backhouse may have been selling these to local hatters. Felt hats were further decorated with a broad ribbon or 'hat band' at the base of the crown. Backhouse had 28 dozen and another 27 hat bands in his inventory. The 'thromed hats' were probably the coarse knitted wool caps worn by working-class men.[34]

33. Cunnington, *Handbook*, pp. 40–7 and 131–42.
34. Cunnington, *Handbook*, p. 137.

Mercers and grocers also sold night caps for men; Backhouse had 'whit capes' (probably plain linen) as well as others of velvet, satin and worsted. Women's coifs were also available and the stock of chapwoman Clarke included 6 plain with accompanying 'crest clothes, 9 coifs of 'black and tawny' and 11 of drawn work, a form of whitework embroidery. Evans stocked this form of women's headwear in considerable numbers: 33 'wrought' (embroidered) coifs, 15 of drawn work and 38 'manchester' coifs, presumably of some form of linen or fustian woven in that Lancashire town. Woodhouse had similar stock: 24 blue coifs (probably calico), 24 drawn-work ones and 2 of silk.

Belts and girdles fastened both men and women's clothing and provided a means of securing purses and tools. Only a few of the entries in inventories give any sort of description; Brat, for example, sold leather girdles and Evans, silk ones. The well-stocked Backhouse had:

> 3 sword girdles, 3s 6d
> 1 dozen girdles, 2s 4d
> 6 belts of leather, 2s ...
> 2 sword girdles buff lether belts, 5s 4d
> 9 yallow single belts, 2s ...
> 6 longe wast girdles of cloth, 18d

Gloves were another essential accessory, for propriety as well as practicality. Those of the wealthy, visible in portraiture and surviving in museum collections, were heavily decorated with ribbons, fringe and embroidery in metal thread. Mercers and grocers sold a limited selection; Brat's inventory listed two dozen of 'cheverell gloves' (kidskin, the finest skin available). Marshall had an extensive variety of kid, cordovan (originally an imported Spanish leather, dyed red), buckskin and sheepskin, in sizes for men, women and children.

Thirsk's description of the knitting industry and its expansion is further supported by hosiers' inventories, as well as those of mercers and grocers. Backhouse had '5 paier of men stockins at 20d a per' and Dennis's inventory listed '2 paire of knit stockines'. In Markland's inventory, categorisation by price, gender and age suggested a degree of sizing:

> 7 pare of Stockinges at 4s 4d
> 6 pare of woolen stockinges at 16d
> 4 pare of stockinges at 3s 6d
> 8 pare of woman's woosted at 2s 6d
> 3 pare woole 2s 4d
> 5 pare woole 2s 2d
> 5 pare for women woole at 15d
> 2 pare Childrens

Stockings were held up with garters; in aristocratic portraits, these are wide strips of fine silk, edged with metal lace and tied in elaborate knots. For the practical purposes of keeping stockings, especially silk ones, from sliding down the leg, a garter of roughly textured wool that would hold both a knot and the stocking, would be required. These can be found in many inventories listed as 'pairs of garters' or 'rolls of gartering'.

The inventories demonstrate that the products of the early economic projects described by Joan Thirsk, particularly bobbin laces, wool fabrics and linens, were available from the middle of the sixteenth century. In addition, these records add another perspective to the 'projects' history by revealing the continued presence of both imports and local manufactures. In the case of linens, competition with imported fabrics remained strong well into the eighteenth century, both the fine versions from France and Holland and the cheaper varieties from Germany, Ireland and Scotland, as well as the white calicos from India. The various fustians, on the other hand, illustrate the development of the Lancashire textile industry to compete with the early Italian and German imports. The broad range of colours available in locally produced cloth provides evidence not only for a more varied palette of rural dress than previously thought, but also for highly skilled dye industries, using local madder, woad and saffron, in addition to imported dyestuffs. Such a range of textiles, trimmings and accessories also indicates a well-developed system of internal transport, conveying not only foreign goods from Bristol and Southampton to Wigan, Winslow and Charlbury, but also the Manchester textiles to Lincoln, Bristol and beyond.

Fashionable clothing or an approximation of it was widely available outside London. Indeed, but for shoes, it would have been possible to dress head to foot from the stocks of Backhouse in 1578 or Marshall in 1665. The goods listed in the mercers' and grocers' inventories suggest ways in which the rural and non-aristocratic population availed themselves of fashionable luxuries. At over £80 in price, a suit embroidered with silver would have been entirely out of reach, but Cowcher's silver buttons, at about 2s a dozen, were not.[35] Even if one could only afford second-hand clothing, these could be easily enhanced and personalised with ribbons, points and decorative fastenings. The small amounts of silk fabric and yards of silk ribbons in the inventories show how this costly luxury accessorised the wardrobes of ordinary people, along with the varieties of inexpensive bobbin laces, wool and linen tapes and fringes, as well as imitation precious-metal trimmings. In the history of dress for the non-élite, the contribution of the second-hand clothing trade is particularly important, but it must be pointed out that the published inventories revealed nothing relating to it. An accident of selection? There remain some million more inventories in manuscript awaiting transcription, and, as this work progresses, perhaps this elusive but essential

35. Strong, 'Charles I's clothes', p. 77.

business will be uncovered. Another avenue of research lies in the details of clothing – colour, fabric, decoration – described in probate inventories and wills beyond those of retailers, to demonstrate in greater detail how and by whom their textile goods were bought and worn.

For historians working with inventories, the foregoing offers useful context and explanations for some of the goods found in the inventories of mercers and grocers. Further analysis of these documents from specific periods and locales will lead to a far more detailed picture than this chapter has been able to present, which would highlight through comparisons how particular regions and communities differed and conformed in materials available for clothing.

Appendix

To avoid repeated footnotes, the inventories referenced in the chapter above are listed in alphabetical order by name.

James Backhouse, grocer, Kirby Lonsdale, Westmorland, 1578: J. Raine (ed.), *Wills and inventories from the registry of the Archdeaconry of Richmond*, Surtees Society, 26 (1853), pp. 275–81.

Edward Brat, mercer, Worcester, Worcestershire, 1552: A.D. Dyer, 'Probate inventories of Worcester tradesmen, 1545–1614', *Worcestershire Historical Society Miscellany II*, new series, 5 (1967), pp. 8–10.

John Browne, woollen-draper, Stratford-upon-Avon, Warwickshire, 1586: J. Jones (ed.), *Stratford-upon-Avon inventories 1538–1699: I: 1538–1625*, Dugdale Society, 39 (2002), pp. 64–74.

Avis Clark, chapwoman, Stratford-upon-Avon, Warwickshire, 1624: Jones (ed.), *Stratford-upon-Avon inventories*, pp. 329–30.

Thomas Cowcher, mercer, Worcester, Worcestershire, 1643: R.G. Griffiths, 'An inventory of the goods and chattels of Thomas Cowcher, mercer, of Worcester, dated 14th November 1643', *Transactions of the Worcestershire Archaeological Society*, new series, 14 (1938), pp. 49–60.

William Davis, chapman, Winslow, Buckinghamshire, 1588: M. Spufford, *The great reclothing of rural England* (London, 1984), pp. 172–7.

Thomas Deakin, shopkeeper, Lichfield, Staffordshire, 1660: D.G. Vaisey (ed.), *Probate inventories of Lichfield and District 1568–1680*, Staffordshire Record Society, 4th series, 5 (1969), pp. 118–20.

Anthony Dennis, shopkeeper, Darlington, Durham, 1611: J.A. Atkinson et al. (eds), *Darlington wills and inventories 1600–1625*, Surtees Society, 201 (1993), pp. 111–22.

Nicholas Elcocke, woollen-draper, Stockport, Cheshire, 1620: C.B. Phillips and J.H. Smith (eds), *Stockport probate records 1620–1650*, Record Society of Lancashire and Cheshire, 131 (1992), pp. 166–71.

James Evans, shopkeeper, Bristol, 1636: E. George and S. George (eds), *Bristol probate inventories, part 1: 1542–1650*, Bristol Record Society, 54 (2002), pp. 98–9.

Richard Gurnell, clothier, Kendal, Westmorland, 1552: Raine (ed.), *Wills and inventories from ... Richmond*, p. 86.

Thomas Harris, mercer, Charlbury, Oxfordshire, 1623: D.G. Vaisey, 'A Charlbury mercer's shop, 1623', *Oxoniensia*, 31–2 (1966–67), pp. 109–16.

Richard Hawkins, woollen-draper, Southampton, Hampshire, 1558: E. Roberts and K. Parker (eds), *Southampton probate inventories 1447–1575, I*, Southampton Record Society, 34 (1992), pp. 120–2.

John Lughting, merchant, Southampton, Hampshire, 1564: Roberts and Parker (eds), *Southampton probate inventories*, pp. 201–23.

Matthew Markland, mercer, Wigan, Lancashire, 1617: J.J. Bagley, 'Matthew Markland, a Wigan mercer: the manufacture and sale of Lancashire textiles in the reigns of Elizabeth I and James I', *Transactions of the Lancashire and Cheshire Antiquarian Society*, 68 (1958), pp. 48–68.

Benjamin Marshall, mercer, Lincoln, Lincolnshire, 1665: J.A. Johnston (ed.), *Probate inventories of Lincoln citizens 1661–1714*, Lincoln Record Society, 80 (1991), pp. 13–21.

Thomas Nelmes, grocer, Bristol, 1634: George and George (eds), *Bristol probate inventories, Part 1*, pp. 83–6.

Richard Thompson, shopkeeper, Richmond, Yorkshire, 1572: Raine (ed.), *Wills and inventories Richmond*, pp. 232–3.

Richard Trendell, chapman, Linge, Norfolk, 1596: Spufford, *The great reclothing of rural England*, pp. 158–60.

James Willinson, mercer, Knaresborough, Yorkshire (1558): Raine (ed.), *Wills and inventories from …
Richmond*, pp. 125–7.

Francis Woodhouse, draper, Chesterfield, Derbyshire: J.M. Bestall and D.V. Fowkes (eds.), *Chesterfield wills and inventories 1604–1650*, Derbyshire Record Society, 28 (2001), pp. 382–4.

Figure 11.1 'Oatcake country': map of the places mentioned in the text
Note: Derbyshire Peak district shaded.

11

Oats and oatcakes: farming
and diet in the north Midlands
in the post-medieval period

MARK DAWSON

One of Joan Thirsk's many contributions to history was to bring out the richness and diversity of English rural life, both in methods of agricultural production and latterly in food consumption.[1] This paper considers an aspect of that diversity: the cultivation of oats as a prime source of human sustenance and their consumption in the form of oatcake. The focus is on the early modern period, but later evidence is used to illustrate traditions often referred to indirectly in earlier records. The geographic scope is the north Midlands, concentrating on northern and western Derbyshire, the area of the modern Peak National Park (see Figure 11.1). The Peak is at the southern end of the Pennine chain, the great upland spine of northern England where throughout the period pastoral forms of agriculture have predominated. The Peak was also at the southern end of what might be termed 'oatcake country' and one of the themes explored here is the relationship between local farming output and diet.

By the sixteenth century oats were a common field crop across the country. They formed an element of human diet in most areas, but their primary use was as a fodder crop. Thomas Cogan and later Gervase Markham both extolled the virtues of oats as human food against literary prejudice inherited from the classical tradition, but such prejudice proved resilient.[2] Dr Johnson famously declared that oats were fed to horses in England and to people in Scotland.[3] As a Staffordshire man, however, he should have known better since oats were the principal bread grain of much of northern England during his lifetime, including parts of his native county. Oats can survive higher rainfall and need lower summer

---

1. J. Thirsk (ed.), *The agrarian history of England and Wales* (hereafter AHEW), 4: 1500–1640 (Cambridge, 1967); J. Thirsk (ed.), AHEW, 5: 1640–1750 (Cambridge, 1985); J. Thirsk, *Food in early modern England: phases, fads and fashions 1500–1760* (London, 2007).
2. T. Cogan, *The haven of health* (London, 1589), pp. 28–9; G. Markham, *The English housewife*, ed. M.R. Best (London, 1994), pp. 199–203.
3. S. Johnson, *Johnson's dictionary: a modern selection*, ed. E.L. McAdam and G. Milne (New York, 1963), p. 268.

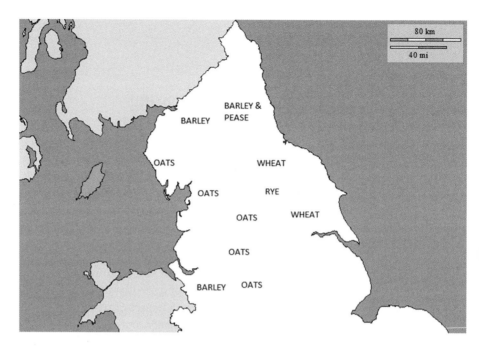

Figure 11.2 Main bread grains of northern England

temperatures than other grains, making them more suited to the poor conditions in large parts of northern England, which were exacerbated by the deteriorating climate in the seventeenth century.

Davies' survey of the diet of the labouring poor in the mid-eighteenth century concluded that across the country nearly two-thirds (63 per cent) ate wheaten bread, 15 per cent rye bread and 12 per cent barley bread. Some 10 per cent ate oats in the form of porridge or oatcakes. Consumption varied with region, so that in the south-east of England 89 per cent ate wheaten bread, whereas in the north the figure was only 30 per cent with a quarter having rye bread and 35 per cent consuming oats in some form. These broad regional figures themselves hide significant variation between one locality and another.[4] The main bread varieties across northern England were noted by Arthur Young in the mid-eighteenth century (Figure 11.2). Wheat bread was mainly confined to the Yorkshire coastal plain. North of the Vale of York rye and wheat were mixed. Northern Northumberland beyond Morpeth to the Scottish border had bread made from a combination of barley and pease, although oatmeal in the form of porridge was also important. In lowland Cumberland, bread was made with oats, barley and

4.   D. Davies, *The case of labourers stated and considered* (London, 1795), quoted in C. Muldrew, *Food, energy and the creation of industriousness: work and material culture in agrarian England 1550–1780* (Cambridge, 2011), p. 60.

rye. Finally, in Westmorland, Lancashire, the Pennine region and into Cheshire, it was oat bread or oatcake that formed the common bread.[5]

Oats provide less energy in terms of calories than other cereals by processed weight but they contain more soluble fibre, making them better at satisfying hunger. Allied to this was the difference in price in the early modern period. Oats were the cheapest grain, on average two-fifths the price of wheat in the period 1640–1750. This made them a cheaper source of calories than wheat and the price difference was even more pronounced in those regions where oats were the main bread grain. In the north and north-west the average price for oats was little over a quarter that of wheat, and across Yorkshire, Derbyshire and Nottinghamshire it ran at around 30 per cent.[6]

Turning to Derbyshire, records from the medieval and early modern periods reveal the importance of oats, particularly in the Peak District. Medieval demesne accounts reveal the primacy of oats and what has been termed almost an 'oat monoculture' on demesnes in the north of the county.[7] Officials of High Peak hundred in 1630 described local grain stocks as 'being chiefly oats and oatmeal, little other grain growing in the said Hundred'.[8] The 1704 tithe account for Carsington, near Wirksworth on the limestone plateau of the southern Peak, lists 128.5 thraves and 9 sheaves of oats with just 21.5 thraves and 1 sheaf of wheat and 10 thraves and 9 sheaves of barley.[9]

Sampled probate inventories for the period 1541–1700, shown in Table 11.1, reveal the differences in grain output between communities in different areas of Derbyshire and neighbouring Nottinghamshire. Over 80 per cent of inventories from Chaddesden and Church Broughton in lowland south Derbyshire record grain, a frequency similar to rural parishes in Nottinghamshire. In the two urban parishes – Chesterfield and Southwell – grain was also commonly listed, and both encompassed large rural hinterlands within their boundaries. Noticeable, however, is the lower frequency of grain recorded in inventories from the two Peak District communities: Brassington and New Mills. The type of grain was also rarely recorded here, suggestive perhaps of the emphasis on pastoral agriculture.[10] Where it was recorded, however, in both places oats appear more often than other

5. The summary of Young's findings comes from W. Kapelle, *The Norman conquest of the north* (London, 1979), p. 214. Kapelle argues that the colonisation of the north was delayed because Norman knights found oats repugnant: pp. 209–30.
6. Thirsk (ed.), *AHEW*, 5, part 2, Tables XVI, XVII, XVIII and XIX, pp. 864–7; Muldrew, *Food, energy and the creation of industriousness*, pp. 142–3.
7. I.S.W. Blanchard, 'Economic change in Derbyshire in the late middle ages, 1272–1540', PhD thesis (London, 1967), pp. 28–9.
8. J. Thirsk and J.P. Cooper (eds), *Seventeenth-century economic documents* (Oxford, 1972), p. 35.
9. Derbyshire Record Office (hereafter DRO), Matlock, D258/7/13/46. A thrave normally contained 24 sheaves.
10. A similar comment is noted in D. Hey, *Derbyshire: a history* (Lancaster, 2008), p. 248.

Table 11.1 Grain recorded in Derbyshire and Nottinghamshire inventories, 1541–1700.

location	number of inventories	% inventories listing					
		grain	oats	barley	wheat	rye	pease
Chaddesden	56	86	18	34	38	21	45
Church Broughton	64	81	13	8	20	2	33
Chesterfield	140	59	32	16	24	11	11
Brassington	51	45	8	4	2	0	0
New Mills	65	58	14	8	3	2	0
Derbyshire average		**66**	**17**	**14**	**17**	**7**	**18**
Southwell	69	54	13	30	29	22	30
Cropwell Bishop	57	79	4	37	26	7	32
East Drayton	53	94	19	83	66	28	85
Misterton	65	86	5	65	60	32	72
Nottinghamshire average		**78**	**10**	**54**	**45**	**22**	**55**

Notes: Inventories sampled for 20-year periods from 1541–1700, excepting 1641–60. Where possible ten inventories were sampled for each period from each place, except Chesterfield where 20 inventories were taken for each period. Chaddesden: E.J. Wheatley, 'Wills and inventories of Chaddesden, Derbyshire 1533 to 1700' (unpublished typescript, Derby Local Studies, 1985); Church Broughton: Lichfield Diocesan Record Office; Chesterfield: J.M. Bestall and D.V. Fowkes (eds), 'Chesterfield wills and inventories 1521–1603', *Derbyshire Record Society*, 1 (1977); J.M. Bestall and D.V. Fowkes (eds), 'Chesterfield wills and inventories 1604–1650', *Derbyshire Record Society*, 28 (2001); 1661–1700 transcripts held in Chesterfield Library, Local Studies; Brassington: transcripts made by Ron Slack and shown to the author; New Mills: R. Bryant, A. Lee and E. Miller (eds), *Wills and inventories of New Mills people, Book One 1540–1571* (Stockport, 1995); R. Bryant, A. Lee and E. Miller (eds), *Wills and inventories of New Mills people, Book Two 1571–1582* (Stockport, 1995); A. Lee and E. Miller (eds), *Wills and inventories of New Mills people, Book Three 1586–1607* (Stockport, 1995); 1607–1700 transcripts held by New Mills Local History Society and shown to the author; Southwell and Cropwell Bishop: Nottinghamshire Archives; East Drayton and Misterton: Borthwick Institute, University of York.

types of crops, as indeed was the case in inventories from the north Derbyshire market town of Chesterfield. By contrast, in Nottinghamshire oats were recorded less often than other types of grain and legumes.

This view of cereal production in Derbyshire is echoed in agricultural surveys from the late eighteenth century. Pilkington said of the High Peak that there was very little grain besides black oats except at Hope, Edensor and Darley in the Derwent valley where they grew wheat and barley.[11] Even in more favourable areas oats dominated. Scarsdale Hundred, in the north-east of the county, has good arable land on magnesian limestone to the east on the Nottinghamshire border, but west of Chesterfield the land rises to over 1,000 feet where the gritstone moorland forms the eastern flank of the Derwent valley. The 1795 crop returns for Scarsdale show that 44 per cent of the arable land was under oats, with 38 per cent wheat, 11 per cent barley and 5 per cent pease.[12] At Rowsley, located on the confluence of the Derwent and Wye, one yeoman farmer in 1761–2 was growing eight acres of oats and around half that each of barley and wheat.[13] It was possible to grow wheat in the Peak, on the right land, but not in sufficient quantity for it to become a staple as it was further south and east.

Like other grains oats were stored on the sheaf and processed when required. Prior to being ground into meal oats had to be dried, particularly when harvested in the often damp Derbyshire weather. Kilns were maintained for this use by communities and also by wealthier landowners who might make them available for their neighbours at a price. The seventeenth-century account books of John Gell of Hopton record receipt of £1 3s 3d for drying 186 sacks of oats.[14] Quarter sessions records reveal the existence of what appears to be a communal or manorial kiln at Edensor, which was broken into and four strikes of oats stolen one night in April 1648 after the dryster had left at dusk. Two decades later, in April 1668, Robert Hollis of Clifton was accused of taking a strike of oats from the kiln of his neighbour, Sir Aston Cockaine. The apparently damning evidence being that a strike of oats was found in Hollis's cow-house when he grew none himself.[15]

The dried oats were ground into meal. Millstones for grinding grain had been quarried from the gritstone edges of the Peak since the late medieval period. John Houghton in 1692 observed that Derbyshire had great quarries of millstones and Defoe noted them being dug from the hillside as he descended to Chatsworth from the 'waste and howling wilderness' of East Moor. Like Derbyshire lead, these were exported through the river port of Bawtry on the Nottinghamshire/Yorkshire

---

11. J. Pilkington, *A view of the present state of Derbyshire*, 1 (London, 1794), pp. 300–1.
12. D.V. Fowkes, 'An analysis of the 1795 crop returns for the Hundred of Scarsdale', *Derbyshire Archaeological Journal*, 115 (1995), p. 152.
13. A. Todd (ed.), *Two years on a Derbyshire farm: the diary of Matthew Gibbons of Rowsley 1761–2* (Bury, 1994), pp. 21–2.
14. DRO, D258/8/15.
15. DRO, Q/SB2/97 and 280.

border. For grinding wheat, millers preferred stones from the Rhineland and Paris basin, but the native Peak millstones were perfectly adequate for inferior grains: oats and barley.[16]

Oats were also processed into malt for use in brewing. Evidence for this is found in a number of records from the medieval period.[17] By the sixteenth century, however, barley malt had come to dominate brewing throughout the country except in the far west of England. Ale brewed with oat malt tasted so disgusting, according to one traveller, that it made visitors sick.[18] Nevertheless, if we are to believe contemporary brewing recipes, an admixture of oats was commonly added, particularly to stronger brews. Gervase Markham's recipe for March beer in *The English Housewife* includes half a peck of oats to a quarter of barley malt to make a hogshead of drink, and William Harrison remarked that his wife used an admixture of oats in her brewing.[19] Given the dominance of oats in north Derbyshire one might expect more widespread use of oats for brewing there. In the late seventeenth century Richard Blome mentioned that oats were occasionally malted and used for beer in Derbyshire, and there is some evidence for this in probate inventories from Chesterfield parish.[20] Thomas Elyott the elder (d.1534) of Walton had 12 strikes of oat malt recorded in his inventory. Agnes Holme (d.1535) had a quarter of malted 'dracheit', probably meaning dredge, a mixture of oats and barley. Henry Sutton (d.1667), baker of Brampton, had ten strikes of oats in his malt house, which may have been stored there ready for processing, although his inventory included a quarter of malt valued at over twice the price per strike of the oats, suggesting that it was barley malt.[21]

In general, however, it seems that the inhabitants of Derbyshire were keen to make up any shortfall they might have had in the barley output of their own county by buying in barley and malt from elsewhere. Derby was famed as a centre for malting; according to Camden its trade was 'to buy corn [grain], and

16. Hey, *Derbyshire*, pp. 199 and 256; D. Hey, *Packmen, carriers and packhorse roads: trade and communications in north Derbyshire and south Yorkshire* (Ashbourne, 2004), p. 101; D. Defoe, *A tour through the whole island of Great Britain*, ed. P. Rogers (London, 1971), p. 476.
17. D.J. Stone, 'The consumption of field crops in late medieval England', in C.M. Woolgar, D. Serjeantson and T. Waldron (eds), *Food in medieval England, diet and nutrition* (Oxford, 2006), p. 18; M. Threlfall-Holmes, *Monks and markets: Durham cathedral priory 1460–1520* (Oxford, 2005), pp. 40–1.
18. R.W. Unger, *Beer in the middle ages and the renaissance* (Philadelphia, 2004), pp. 158, 161; C. Dyer, 'Did the peasants really starve in medieval England?', in M. Carlin and J. Rosenthal (eds), *Food and eating in medieval Europe* (London, 1998), pp. 57–8.
19. Markham, *The English housewife*, p. 207; W. Harrison, *The description of England*, ed. G. Edelen (New York, 1994), p. 138.
20. From R. Blome, *Britannia* (1673), quoted in G.E. Fussell, 'Four centuries of farming systems in Derbyshire: 1500–1900', *Derbyshire Archaeological Journal*, 71 (1951), p. 14.
21. Bestall and Fowkes (eds), *Chesterfield wills and inventories 1521–1603*, pp. 4–7; Chesterfield Local Studies (hereafter CLS), inventory transcript of Henry Sutton.

having turn'd it into Malt, to sell it again to the highland counties'. There were 70 malthouses recorded in the borough in 1693, and William Woolley described the town's principal trade in the early eighteenth century as malting.[22] As the probate inventory evidence presented earlier suggests, large quantities of barley were grown in neighbouring Nottinghamshire. Philip Kinder in his manuscript history of the county written c.1663 wrote that Derbyshire folk got most of their barley and malt from Nottingham and Loughborough. In 1640 the White Peak lead-mining centre of Wirksworth was said to gain most of its malt from Derby as well as Mansfield, Nottingham and other 'remote places'.[23] Far from making her sick, Celia Fiennes, visiting the north of the county in 1698, found in Chesterfield 'the best ale in the kingdom generally esteem'd' and Daniel Defoe was similarly impressed with the ale in Wirksworth.[24] It seems likely, therefore, that barley malt formed the basis of most drink brewed in Derbyshire in the early modern period.

Whilst the evidence suggests that brewing was firmly centred on malted barley, it is clear that across northern England even by the mid-eighteenth century there was still a wide variance in the grains used for baking. Our focus now turns to the uses of oats and oatmeal as food, particularly in the form of oatcakes and the particular style of oatcakes baked in northern and western Derbyshire. Throughout the country oatmeal formed a thickener in the ubiquitous pottage, seemingly to be found bubbling away in every English home. Andrew Boorde declared that 'Potage is nat so much used in al Christendom as it is used in Englande.'[25] Oats and oatmeal were also used to make porridge and to bulk out puddings, but a greater variety of these seems to have existed in those areas where oats dominated. William Ellis, writing in the mid-eighteenth century, noted burgoo made with fine oatmeal and milk, or sometimes water, and known in Derbyshire as thin pudding. Another Derbyshire recipe was lumpy-tums, clumps of oatmeal dropped into boiling water.[26] What set apart those areas where oats dominated from the rest of England, however, was their use of oatmeal to make various forms of oat bread or oatcakes.

Sambrook, in her study of Staffordshire oatcakes, suggests oat breads were being baked before the Norman Conquest, citing as evidence the Old English origin of the word bakestone and the use of the Norse word *haver*, meaning oats, in compounds such as haversack and havercake. She also delineates two basic

22. Hey, *Derbyshire*, pp. 222 and 275; C. Glover and P. Riden (eds), *William Woolley's history of Derbyshire*, Derbyshire Record Society, 6 (Chesterfield, 1981), p. 23.

23. P. Kinder, 'Historie of Darby-shire', transcribed by W.G.D. Fletcher, *The Reliquary*, 22 (1881–2), p. 23; Hey, *Derbyshire*, p. 240.

24. C. Morris, *The illustrated journeys of Celia Fiennes 1685–c.1712* (London, 1995), p. 104; Defoe, *Tour*, p. 460.

25. A. Boorde, *A compendyous regyment of a dyetary for helth* (London, 1542), fo. G1.

26. W. Ellis, *The country housewife's companion*, p. 265; N.E. Toft, 'Some Derbyshire dishes and Derbyshire ways', *The Derbyshire Countryside*, 14 (1934), p. 35.

sorts of oat bread made in northern England.[27] The first, as found in Yorkshire, Lancashire and the Lakeland counties, was made with stiff dough thrown or clapped onto a board and then baked. These breads were variously termed clapbread, havercake or haverbread. Once cooked, they were hung to dry on a rack called a fleak, after which they would last for many months. Ellis was clearly thinking of this type when he wrote of meal used in the northern counties:

> Here they make vast consumption of oatmeal, having but little wheat growing in these parts, and with this they make cakes that supply bread, by mixing oatmeal with water and a little salt, which they let stand together twenty or more hours, and then knead it into a dough or batter, and bake it like pancakes on a stone that has a fire under it; and when they have prepared a good parcel, they lay them on racks to dry, for in this manner they become hard, and will keep hard, sweet, and sound a long time.[28]

The second type was made with a thinner pouring dough or batter, usually containing some form of raising agent, either barm from brewing or soured with the leftover dough or batter from a previous batch. This was the type that was made in the north midlands – Staffordshire, Derbyshire and neighbouring areas of south Yorkshire – what might be termed the 'southern oatcake zone'.[29] For the making of this second type of oatcake we have a detailed account provided by Farey in his early nineteenth-century agricultural survey of Derbyshire, describing the method of baking oatcakes he observed at Mr Joseph Gould's farm at Pilsbury on the Staffordshire border. No yeast or barm was used but instead what Farey calls an acid fermentation 'excited' in leaven or batter made in a sour wooden tub called a doshen. These oatcakes were made by applying the sour-dough principle, using the leftovers from the previous batch. The doshen was never washed in winter but in summer it was rinsed with cold water. The batter was described as thicker than that for pancakes and was poured onto a bakestone, being spread with the back of a wooden ladle to around a quarter-inch thick and 16 to 18 inches round. After about a minute and a half of baking a cake slice was used to release the oatcake from the bakestone and a bake sprittle or cake board was used to flip it over. After a further two and a half minutes it was turned again and after two and half minutes more it was removed and draped on an earthenware dish to steam whilst another was made, before then being transferred to a pile on a board.[30]

The second method of making oatcakes seems to have prevailed across the southern oatcake zone. Descriptions of oatcake baking collected in the 1940s by

27. P. Sambrook, *The Staffordshire oatcake: a history* (Lancaster, 2009), pp. 19 and 26.
28. Ellis, *Country housewife's companion*, p. 53.
29. P. Brears, 'Oatcake in the West Riding', *Folk Life*, 12 (1974), pp. 55–9 describes both types of oatcake being made in west and south Yorkshire.
30. J. Farey, *General view of the agriculture and minerals of Derbyshire*, 2 (London, 1813), p. 130.

Table 11.2 Baking equipment in Derbyshire inventories, 1541–1700.

location	bakestones, doshens and sprittles		total with baking equipment *	
	number	%	number	%
Chaddesden	–	–	14	25
Church Broughton	–	–	7	11
Chesterfield	13	9	34	24
Brassington	3	6	5	10
New Mills	5	8	6	9

Note:* Defined as boulting tubs, kneading troughs, peals and ovens as well as bakestones, doshens and sprittles.

Source: See Table 11.1.

a Yorkshire physician, Dr Thomas Bedford, reveal a tradition of making oatcakes in the Sheffield area using a dough or batter poured onto a bakestone and turned with a wooden sprittle. Sambrook found similar descriptions for the Staffordshire moorlands and the presence of bakestones, back sprittles and doshens in seventeenth-century probate inventories suggests the method had not changed much over the centuries.[31]

Probate inventories from northern and western Derbyshire also reveal these items associated with oatcake baking and their incidence is recorded in Table 11.2 together with the incidence of all types of baking equipment. Virtually all the baking equipment in the Brassington and New Mills inventories were items associated with oatcake baking, although Thomas Westerne (d.1622), a gentleman from Brassington, had a kneading trough and boulting tub, suggesting he, at least, had more regular types of bread produced in his household. Chesterfield parish seemingly straddled the edge of oatcake country with a mixture of baking equipment recorded, sometimes within the same household. Robert Turner (d.1681), yeoman of Linacre, had a doshen, but also a kneading trough and an iron peal. Similarly, Abraham Cundy (d.1686), miller of Holymoorside, had a doshen and a kneading trough in his kitchen.[32]

Bakestones could either be made of stone or of metal (see Figure 11.3), indeed inventories from the New Mills area refer to bread irons rather than bakestones. Robert Arnefield (d.1580), yeoman of Broadhurst, had a bread 'yrene' worth 5s

31. University of Leeds, Brotherton Library, Special Collections (hereafter ULSC), MS423/4; Sambrook, *Staffordshire oatcake*, p. 45.
32. CLS, inventory transcripts of Robert Turner and Abraham Cundy.

Figure 11.3 A hanging
iron bakestone
Source: Photograph
courtesy of Bakewell Old
House Museum.

and Richard Sylvester (d.1597) of Hoole Croft House owned a bread iron.[33] Farey
writing in the early nineteenth century observed the stone varieties as being thin
and round, set in a frame hanging from the pothook over the fire in commoners'
cottages, or larger and square for setting over a stove in the more substantial
households. The bakestones were quarried from local Millstone grit at several
locations in the eastern part of Peak, but over in the north-west at Bakestone
Clough, near Glossop, they were made of shale three-quarters of an inch thick
and 15 to 16 inches wide. The tradition of quarrying and shaping bakestones in
this particular area is recorded in the sixteenth century.[34] As with other items
associated with baking, both doshens and bakestones tend to be mentioned in the

33. Bryant *et al.* (eds), *New Mills people, Book Two*, pp. 19–22; Lee and Miller (eds), *New Mills people, Book Three*, pp. 30–4.

34. J. Farey, *General view of the agriculture and minerals of Derbyshire*, 1 (London, 1811), pp. 431–44; Brears, 'Oatcake', pp. 57–8 maps the locations of bakestone quarries in west and south Yorkshire.

household inventories of the wealthier husbandmen and yeomen farmers, such as Joseph Gould, where they were used to bake in bulk both for the household and hungry farm workers. However, relatively few inventories actually mention doshens. This may have been because they were hard to distinguish from other tubs and vessels in the deceased's home, differing in their use rather than their form. Perhaps it was only the presence of some residual oatcake batter that served to identify the particular use of a tub and hence to suggest to the appraisers the particular word to use to describe it.[35]

Bakestones with their specific form should not suffer from similar issues of recording, but they like doshens appear infrequently. In this case part of the answer may be that a bakestone was not needed to bake oatcakes. In the late sixteenth century Dr Jones wrote of 'Bread cakes like the oatcakes in Kendal that are cooked on irons, or on Slat [slate] stones as in High Peak or on frying pans as in Derbyshire'.[36] There were clearly alternatives, therefore, for those households with more limited cooking equipment, and the humble and ubiquitous frying pan may often have doubled as a bakestone.

Of course, as with other types of bread-baking, not every household baked their own oatcakes. Only around half the inventories from New Mills and Brassington list grain, and when we consider that surviving inventories in general are skewed towards the middle ranks of early modern society, including those with a more substantial landholding or stake in agriculture, it is likely that only a minority of households had their own supplies of oats. There were probably many like Robert Hollis who grew no oats, and their numbers would have expanded when we consider the increasing numbers of landless lead-miners in the Peak District in the seventeenth century.[37] These people were likely to have bought rather than baked their oatcakes.

The author Alison Uttley, recalling her childhood in Derbyshire at the turn of the twentieth century, mentions the itinerant oatcake man selling at the door, and within the inventories we can identify his forebears.[38] The inventory of Anne Lane (d.1674), widow of Brassington, lists a bakehouse with two bakestones and a bake sprittle, suggesting she may have been baking oatcakes on a commercial scale. That of her neighbour, baker Jonathan Hill (d.1689), interestingly lists none of the peals, kneading troughs and other paraphernalia usually associated with his trade. Instead he had a hut and a 'harth stone' and it seems highly likely that he baked oatcakes on this stone in his hut. The inventory of Henry Sutton (d.1667), baker of

35. See B. Trinder, 'The wooden horse in the cellar: words and contexts in Shropshire probate inventories', in T. Arkell, N. Evans and N. Goose (eds), *When death do us part: understanding and interpreting the probate records of early modern England* (Oxford, 2004), pp. 274–9 for a similar discussion of local terms used for coopery ware.
36. J. Jones, *The benefit of the auncient bathes of Buckstones* (London, 1572), p. 9.
37. A. Wood, *The politics of social conflict: the Peak country 1520–1770* (Cambridge, 1999), p. 66.
38. A. Uttley, *Old farmhouse recipes* (Barnsley, 2010), p. 56.

Brampton near Chesterfield offers more insight. Sutton had a 'backstone to bake oate bread' giving clear evidence of this practice, but he also had two kneading troughs and a moulding board as well as the stone for his oven valued at 5s.[39] Like Robert Turner and Abraham Cundy, both also from settlements to the west of Chesterfield, Sutton was baking oatcakes as well as more regular types of bread.

Derbyshire oatcakes were substantial items as the dimensions quoted earlier would suggest. The household accounts for the Earls of Rutland at Haddon Hall list the purchase of oatcakes at 3d each from Robert Broomehead's wife for workers fetching coal in 1664. Given that Arthur Young recorded oatbread being sold in Leeds a century later at a penny for 10 or 11 ounces, these Derbyshire oatcakes could have been in excess of two pounds or more in weight.[40] There is an interesting parallel here between the large size of Derbyshire oatcakes and the size of other types of bread. William Ellis relates information from one of his correspondents, a former servant of his latterly employed as a ploughman by a Derbyshire gentry family, who were said to bake loaves using a peck of flour that were left to 'sweeten' in the oven overnight. It was doubtless such a sizeable loaf, valued at 1s 8d, which was stolen from the oven of Thomas Nuthall of Stanton near Youlgreave in 1648.[41]

The size of oatcakes and loaves may have reflected restricted supplies of fuel, particularly in the White Peak where woodland was limited, with much wood reserved for industrial uses and field boundaries formed of dry-stone walls rather than hedgerows. Those that baked oatcakes may also have made them in bulk for similar reasons. Mrs Gill of Brierlow Farm near Ashbourne, interviewed by Bedford in the 1940s, recalls her own grandmother baking oatcakes once a week, making a stack a foot to 18 inches high of around 50 cakes, each a foot to 18 inches in diameter.[42]

Oatcake was apparently enjoyed by the local inhabitants in Derbyshire. Kinder in the seventeenth century wrote that 'The common inhabitants doe preferr Oates for delight and strength above any other graine'. His opinion was echoed a century and a half later by Sir Humphrey Davy, who in 1813 wrote that 'The Derbyshire miners in winter prefer oatcakes to wheaten bread ... such nourishment enables them to support their strength and perform their labours better'. Mrs Gill recalled that oatcakes were generally toasted before eating and that her mother had an iron bakestone, but they always tasted best when baked on a stone one – a preference

39. R. Slack, *Lands and lead miners: a history of Brassington in Derbyshire* (Stroud, 2007), p. 63; transcript of inventory of Jonathan Hill transcribed by Ron Slack; CLS, inventory transcript of Henry Sutton.

40. Manuscript transcript of Haddon Household accounts made by W.A. Carrington 1895–6, p. 393, viewed by permission of Trevor Brighton; A. Young, *A six months tour through the north of England*, 1 (London, 1771), p. 139.

41. Ellis, *Country housewife's companion*, pp. 249–50; DRO, Q/SB2/101.

42. ULSC, MS423/4.

that Farey also recorded a century earlier.[43] Further information comes from another two of Bedford's interviewees from Middleton, near Youlgreave. Mrs Brookes baked her oatcakes on a slab of gritstone, using a 'becksprittle' to turn them. Elderly neighbours, she said, had oatcakes most of the time, with white bread only on Sundays. Her neighbour, Mrs Cooper, likewise said her parents had oatcakes most of the time and white bread only on Sundays. She also stated that oatcakes were eaten toasted except by the children who would occasionally have them soft with treacle.[44]

The opinion of outsiders was often less positive, however. Farey in the early nineteenth century, rather disparagingly, said the people of Derbyshire live comfortably 'notwithstanding that nearly all their bread' in the north in particular was oatcakes, of a 'thin, soured, soft kind'. The harsh experience of a young London apprentice, John Birley, sent to work at Litton Mill, near Tideswell, in 1810, started when he was given Derbyshire oatcake on his arrival, which he and his fellows could not eat, despite their hunger, because it was 'sour as vinegar'. The torture continued when in addition to the long hours they had to endure breakfast consisting of water-porridge, with oatcake in it and onions for flavour. Dinner consisted of Derbyshire oatcakes cut into four pieces, arranged into two stacks: one buttered and the other 'treacled'. Birley's experience was paralleled by that of his near contemporary Robert Blincoe, whose biographer John Brown adopted a similar disdainful view of oatcakes.[45] The negative opinions of oatcakes expressed in these nineteenth-century sources are also suggested in earlier centuries. The sixteenth-century household accounts of the Willoughby family reveal oatcakes being purchased during Lent for their household at Middleton, on the Warwickshire/Staffordshire border in the 1520s and at Wollaton, near Nottingham in the 1590s. This is also seen in the accounts from 1585 of the Francis family of Foremark in south Derbyshire.[46] Was it the case that for these wealthy gentry families consuming the peasant food of neighbouring areas to the north and west was a form of penance?

The presence of oatcake in these elite households outside oatcake country should also alert us to the difficulties of trying to draw neat lines on a map, whether for the purposes of delineating patterns of agricultural production, or of food consumption. Examples from inventories quoted earlier reveal households

43. Kinder, 'Darby-shire', p. 21; Davy quoted in J. Douglas, *Old Derbyshire recipes and customs* (Nelson, 1976), p. 3; ULSC, MS423/4.
44. ULSC, MS423/4.
45. J. Farey, *General view of the agriculture and minerals of Derbyshire*, 3 (London, 1817), p. 624; Birley's account appeared in *The Ashton Chronicle* 19 May 1849, <http://spartacus-educational.com/IRbirley.htm>, accessed 15 February 2015; J. Brown, *A Memoir of Robert Blincoe* (London, 1832), pp. 32–4.
46. M. Dawson, *Plenti and grase: food and drink in a sixteenth-century household* (Totnes, 2009), pp. 69–70; DRO, D156 M/A4 fo. 27v.

Figure 11.4 Derbyshire oatcakes –
an enduring tradition
Note: Modern Derbyshire oatcakes
are thicker than Staffordshire
ones, but a fraction of the size of
their forerunners.
Source: Author.

where both oatcakes and more regular loaves were being baked and presumably also consumed. As well as being a centre for malting, Derby bakers in the early eighteenth century were supplying bread to the inhabitants of the Peak, with Wirksworth in particular acting as a market for their wares.[47] Wheaten bread was clearly available as an alternative in northern and western Derbyshire from at least the seventeenth century if not before. Did the 'common inhabitants' of Kinder's day buy it for eating on Sundays as they did in more recent times?

It is an attractive picture to see the cultivation of oats and the baking of oatcakes as a natural synthesis of climate and geology: the grain suited for the damp climate, ground into meal using millstones and baked on bakestones both quarried from local hillsides. It appealed to the early nineteenth-century writers such as Farey and it appeals to us now, but it ignores human agency. Taste, in both a cultural and a culinary context, has a major role to play, because humans unlike animals do not simply consume the food that is growing around them. From Kinder through to the people interviewed by Bedford in the 1940s there is a sense that oatcakes were bound up with identity, something that helps keep the tradition of oatcake-baking alive today (see Figure 11.4). There is also evidence to suggest that their consumption was an expression of preference. The taste for barley malt was clearly established in Derbyshire by the seventeenth century if not earlier, and the county developed a reputation for brewing good beer. Wheaten bread on the other hand never became the staple it was elsewhere, still reported as an occasional treat in parts of the county in the early twentieth century. For locals it was probably a treat to try something different on a Sunday, a day of rest, but when there was work to do there was nothing to beat an oatcake.

---

47. Glover and Riden (eds), *Woolley's history of Derbyshire*, p. 177.

12

Peter Walkden and the
world of goods

RICHARD HOYLE

So far as I am aware, Joan Thirsk never encountered the diary of Peter Walkden except through a paper I wrote and sent her some years ago. Had she written about Walkden, she would doubtless have done it better than I can, but I am sure she would have enjoyed this paper, touching, as it does, on clothes and food.[1]

Peter Walkden was a nonconformist clergyman, a farmer and diarist who, in the 1730s, lived a few miles to the north-east of Preston in Lancashire. From there he moved to a chapel at Holcombe near Bury in 1738, and then he moved again to minister to a congregation in Southport where he died in 1769. Throughout his life he appears to have kept a diary, the one extant volume of which covers a 14-month period of his life when he was living near Chipping, ministering to a congregation in Newton in Bowland and, as explained in an earlier paper, pursuing a rather odd dual economy as a farmer and minister.[2] The diary, which extends to a little over 450 pages of printed text, is the fullest account we have of what it was like to be a small farmer, or perhaps to live amongst, the small farmers of central Lancashire in the early eighteenth century.[3] Moreover, Walkden used his diary as an aide-mémoire of his income and expenditure. It is easy – if tedious – to turn the diary into accounts. Once done, it is possible to show that the chapel barely paid its way, but Walkden received occasional gifts from the London-based nonconformist charities. In July 1733 he had £8 3s from two charity funds in London: how he

1. Joan, of course, wrote on many of the consumables of the woman's sphere in her *Economic policy and projects: the development of a consumer society in early modern England* (Oxford, 1981) and by doing so invented a branch of history. Her last book was the pioneering *Food in early modern England* (London, 2007).
2. R.W. Hoyle, 'Farmer, nonconformist minister and diarist: the world of Peter Walkden of Thornley in Lancashire, 1733–34', *Northern History*, 48 (2011), pp. 271–94.
3. Chipping Local History Society, *The diary of the Reverend Peter Walkden for 1733–1734* (Chipping, 2000), hereafter cited as *Diary*. Biographical details are taken from the *Diary*, pp. xviii–xix. There is a badly out-of-date biography in ODNB. Extracts from the diary reproduced here are given in modernised spelling.

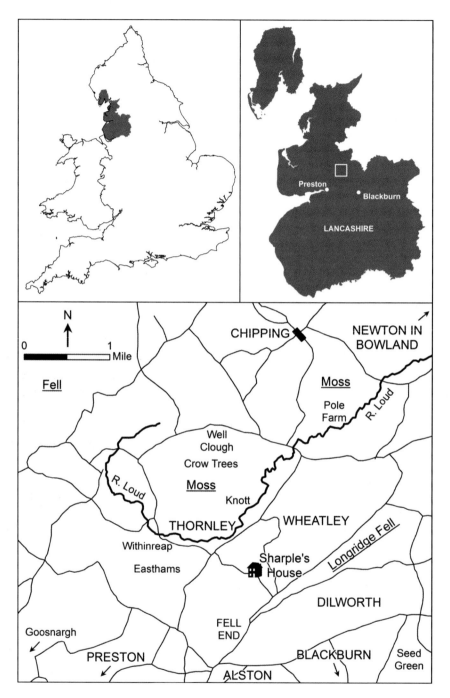

Figure 12.1 The area around Thornley-with-Wheatley (Lancashire) showing the location of places mentioned in this article, including Walden's farm, which is identified by the Chipping Local History Society as the modern Sharple's House.

spent this money is terribly revealing of the family's aspirations as consumers.[4] He borrowed a great deal and ran into a major liquidity crisis during the duration of the diary which he could only resolve by borrowing further. As a farmer he grew oats and potatoes, apparently for the use of the household rather than sale, but it was the income from his London patrons which allowed him to spend much of the day sitting in his closet, reading, writing up his diary and transcribing into it copious extracts from newspapers and other printed materials that passed through his hands.

At this time the Walkden household consisted of eight members including a resident farm boy and, for a few weeks, a young woman employed by Walkden's wife. Catherine Walkden was his second wife: she appears in the diary as 'my love'. He had two sons by his first wife, the elder of whom, Thomas, was working in Blackburn as a weaver of checked cloth. Walkden's second son was in service locally, but he returned home when his health broke down for a period. Walkden's daughter by his first marriage, Margaret, was still at home aged around 17. Walkden's elder child by his second marriage, Henry, was only 12 years old when the diary opens and was also living at home. His father was paying for him to go to school and at the end of 1732 Peter and Catherine heard him parse and were well satisfied as to his learning. In time Henry became a nonconformist minister like his father. Peter and Catherine's three younger daughters, the youngest only three when the diary opened, were still at home and at school. Walkden and his wife were helped by a local lad, Harry Wilkinson, who lived with the Walkdens and over the year of the diary got into more than one scrape. As we shall see, Catherine Walkden seems to have been fairly autonomous in her activities, keeping the profits of her dairying and poultry to spend on her own purposes.

This then, is the core *dramatis personae*. The other figures who appear repeatedly in the diary are the local farmers and shopkeepers of Thornley and what Walkden refers to as Fell End, the hamlet which is now incorporated into the small town of Longridge (Figure 12.1). Fell End had an alehouse run by Ellen Seed, a shop selling haberdashery and candles (Thomas Eccles), a butcher (John Brown) and a cobbler. But for bigger purchases the Walkdens went to Preston. This paper considers the Walkden family's role as consumers, an aspect omitted from my earlier paper.

Consumption in the diary

It is now recognised that the first half of the eighteenth century saw the introduction into England of a whole range of new products, and yet it is not

---

4.   Diary, 24 July.

clear that the Walkdens drank from the cup of novelty.[5] The first to become commonplace was tobacco. There was then sugar – far from unknown in England in the seventeenth century, but with the opening up of the West Indies transformed from an expensive product into a fairly cheap consumable. The rise of cheap sugar was associated with the appearance of three imported drinks which, to a greater or lesser extent, needed sugar to make them palatable: tea, coffee and chocolate. The variety of household furnishings increased, including the appearance of domestic clocks, mirrors and looking glasses, and new Chinese crockery (and its imitators). In clothing new Indian and cotton fabrics became available. In a real sense consumers had available to them a much wider range of goods in the 1730s than it had been possible to buy a half-century before, certainly a century before. Moreover, the indications are that these products were widely distributed, which is not to say that everyone had the financial means to enter this new world of goods. The same period saw the beginnings of a great elaboration of retailing, with the proliferation of shops in the countryside.[6]

It has been suggested that the enlargement of the range of manufactured products available for purchase and their attractiveness encouraged households to re-orientate their work towards earning more income, which could then be spent on the acquisition of these goods.[7] There was, then, a tension between leisure and the expansion of income, with the former being foregone to allow the purchase of goods which were socially desirable. Hence households had to move beyond self-sufficiency to being acquisitive in order to display the right goods and furnishings, and extend their consumption.

Much of our knowledge of the adoption of these new products comes from probate inventories. Of course, this is not without its problems. Many inventories come from the elderly and socially conservative at the end of their lives. Moreover, the practice of making inventories – or at least the practice of the church courts of retaining inventories – seems to have run down about this time. The search is therefore on for sources which show not what people had acquired by the end of

5.   The literature on these issues is now too large to be quickly summarised in a footnote, and perhaps too familiar to require one. But for an inventory-based study of Goosnargh, within a few miles of Fell End, which considers the social significance of possessions, see H. French, *The middle sort of people in provincial England, 1620–1750* (Oxford, 2002). For a useful discussion of the new consumables, see Jon Stobart, *Sugar and spice: grocers and groceries in provincial England, 1659–1830* (Oxford, 2013), chapter 1. For clothing, see John Styles, *The dress of the people: everyday fashion in eighteenth-century England* (London, 2007).

6.   Stobart, *Sugar and spice*; J. Stobart, 'Food retailers and rural communities: Cheshire butchers in the long eighteenth century', *Local Population Studies*, 79 (2007), pp. 23–36; J. Stobart and A. Hann, 'Retailing revolution in the eighteenth-century: evidence from north-west England', *Business History*, 46 (2004), pp. 171–94.

7.   J. De Vries, *The industrious revolution: consumer behaviour and the household economy, 1650 to the present* (Cambridge, 2008).

their lives (or rather, *retained* to the end of their lives) and were deemed valuable enough to be worthy of recording, but sources which show in real time what people were spending their money on, the how and where they made purchases, as well as the question of what they purchased. So, attention has switched from inventories towards accounts.[8] The advantage of the Walkden diary though is that it gives purchases a context that allows us to understand the choice that was made when they were purchased. Moreover, it also allows us to see their purchases of products which normally escape attention, certainly in inventory studies – notably meat, where Gritt, using the account book of another Lancashire farmer of this period, Robert Latham, has shown that there is a story to be told of the choices people made in the meat they ate.[9]

We do have to acknowledge one key difficulty with the diary as a source. As a diarist, Walkden was uninterested in the daily routine of the women in the household: indeed, he comes over as strangely detached from what was going on about him. For example, the day they slaughtered the pig, they ran out of saltpetre; whilst more was being fetched, Walkden returned to his closet to continue writing up his account of the day so far.[10] An equally telling episode comes when, in March 1734, the slaughtered pig's successor went missing. This was a Sunday so Walkden started the day by saying prayers in the chapel, then he and Catherine went to the alehouse, after which they went home, Walkden stopping to do so some business on the way.

> Got in about 2 o'clock and found our pig had got out of its coat [sty] and was gone: my Love [Catherine Walkden] went in search of it but I went into my lodging room and continued the account of the day thus far. So went down and enquired after my Love and the pig. But they found it not. Then went out again and heard of it being at Bartle Eccles of the Knott, and William Eccles of Johns came and told me it was there too and I sent Henry and Margaret for it: and my Love came home first, and Margaret, Henry and Harry came with the pig.[11]

There is no sign that Walkden himself went looking for the pig!

---

8. J. Whittle and E. Griffiths, *Consumption and gender in the early seventeenth-century household: the world of Alice le Strange* (Oxford, 2012); Styles, *Dress of the people*, draws heavily on accounts; D. Tankard, 'Giles Moore's clothes: the clothing of a Sussex rector, 1656–1679' (forthcoming).
9. A.J. Gritt, 'The farming and domestic economy of a Lancashire smallholder: Richard Latham and the agricultural revolution, 1724–67', in R. W. Hoyle (ed.), *The farmer in England, 1650–1980* (Farnham, 2013), pp. 101–34. Styles has also analysed the clothing of the Latham family in detail: *Dress of the people*, passim, but especially pp. 229–45.
10. Diary, 12 February 1734.
11. Diary, 10 March 1734.

It is clear that the Walkdens kept animals – Peter usually began the day by foddering them – and that Catherine Walkden and her daughters both milked and made butter. Catherine normally went to Preston on a Saturday to sell the butter; occasionally, she also took chickens. Walkden seems to have allowed the income she made from these activities to remain in her hands, and, although it is never quite said, it seems probable that she spent it on a mixture of household needs and clothing for herself and her daughters. On the occasions Walkden went with her to a shop, either in Preston or one of the local shops at Fell End, he normally paid. He also seems to have settled the book debts that accumulated with local shopkeepers. On one occasion, in his absence, Catherine took money from his closet; Walkden noticed its absence on his return and had her explain how she had spent it. But, overall, it seems likely that Catherine was allowed a great deal more latitude to trade on her own, and to her own advantage, than some of the other married woman we learn about in the diary.[12]

The consequence is that that diary does not record all the commercial transactions to which the household was party. Catherine, as we noted, went to Preston weekly, but the diary never gives a hint of how much she made there, and, except for casual references to things that she bought there, never records how she spent her earnings. A total assessment is therefore made impossible by the division of responsibilities in the household. Nonetheless, we can go a good distance, but what we tend to learn about is Peter Walkden rather than his wife and children.

We can also note a second weakness with the diary as a source. Walkden never tells us what he ate. We can speculate that the household lived largely off oats in various forms, including oatcakes (see chapter 11), which remained popular in this part of Lancashire, and potatoes.[13] We can speculate a little about the family's consumption of meat, but Walkden never once tells us what his wife placed on the table before him. In such ways do even the finest sources have their lacunae.

Purchases of new goods

In fact the penetration of new goods into the Walkden household seems fairly slight. They certainly used sugar. On one occasion Peter Walkden bought a pound of sugar from Richard Dilworth and paid for a pound that his wife had bought 'some time ago', which makes it sound as though the family were not big sugar consumers.[14] On another occasion they bought treacle, although we get no clue

12. Hoyle, 'World of Peter Walkden', p. 276.
13. Celia Fiennes noted that she encountered oat bread for the first time when going north at Garstang, 10 miles past Preston: C. Fiennes, *The Journeys of Celia Fiennes*, ed. C. Morris (London, 1947), p. 188, also Thirsk, *Food in early modern England*, pp. 219–20.
14. *Diary*, 8 October. This seems to be one of the few times that they shopped at Dilworth's (they bought salt off him on 25 June), although he was a member of Walkden's congregation. It might be noted that Walkden also kept bees, e.g. *Diary*, 6 September, 26 October.

as to its use.[15] There is no sign that they drank coffee, tea or chocolate, but Peter Walkden at least was well committed to tobacco and bought it both locally and in quite large packages from Preston.[16] To all appearances the Walkdens were located in a traditional society of alehouse sociability. What is perhaps more surprising is that, both there and at home, they seem to have drunk brandy (although when they went to Preston, they drank ale). Smoking was closely connected with the social life of the alehouse, but the newer drinks were not, and we have to assume that whatever use the Walkdens had for sugar it was in cooking rather than to make drinks palatable. Sugar appears again a couple of times when the Walkdens bought toffee in Preston and brought it home for their children as treats: these were the occasions on which they felt they had money to spare after grants from the nonconformist charities.[17]

Another form of new goods which Peter Walkden bought regularly was news. He had a weekly newspaper (from which he transcribed much material into his diary) from Ellen Seed the alehouse keeper, brought to him by his son. Walkden appears to have kept them for a couple of days before they were taken back. In return for this service he paid Ellen a fee for the loan of the papers, as on 22 March, 'and son Henry going to school, I sent the newspaper and 3d for the news I have had since Christmas last, to Ellen Seed'. In this context it is worth remarking that Walkden was also paying for the education of his children. His son Henry's tuition cost 10s a year (and in addition 3s for three weeks' summer teaching in arithmetic) and that of his younger daughters 6s a year (paid quarterly) each.[18]

Meat consumption

So, if the Walkdens seem not to have indulged in the new commercial products, then what about meat, a product which was available locally in abundance? All the Walkden's purchases of meat in the first twelve months of the diary are summarised in Table 12.1.[19]

The consumption of meat by the Walkdens cannot be disentangled from their relationship with the local butcher and slaughterman, John Brown. (Brown also did other tasks for the Walkdens, including gelding animals). As keepers of livestock, the Walkdens had the option of either slaughtering their own animals or selling them

15. *Diary*, 30 April. It may have been used for cattle rather than human consumption.
16. There are 14 references to the purchase of tobacco in the diary for February 1733 to January 1734. On four occasions, he bought bulk tobacco in Preston (or Catherine bought it for him), as much as 8 pounds at 8d the pound on one occasion (*Diary*, 24 February, 28 July, 1 December and 22 December): this was 12 pounds over the year. Twice he bought tobacco of Thomas Eccles but only quarterns when funds were low (*Diary*, 30 April, 21 November). On the remaining eight occasions, he bought 'papers' of tobacco in alehouses.
17. *Diary*, 4 August, 8 September.
18. *Diary*, 12 April, 22 September, 15 October, 10 December, 21 January 1734.
19. References to the following section can be found in Table 12.1.

Table 12.1 *Purchases of meat by Peter and Catherine Walkden, February 1733–January 1734.*

1733		
12 March	John Brown	'I payd Ann Brown 2d 2 qrs for ye calf feet etc we had last Saturday of her husband and she said ye wod Kill another next wednesday which we might then fetch'.
15 March	John Brown	[The frost kept the Lad from harrowing until 10 o'clock], 'before which hour he fetchted ye calve feet and belly from John Browns'. [Later in the day] 'came thence to Ellen Seeds and finding John Brown there, he profferd me a shoulder of veal, it sticking on his hand: I bou[gh]t it of him and paid him 1s for it and the feet and belly we had today. So he is payd for all we have had of him'.
12 May	John Brown	'John Brown willd me to buy some veal of him: I told him if [it] stickt on his hands I wo[ul]d take some ... [we] brought with us a shoulder of veal from Brown's'.
18 May	John Brown	'About noon came John Brown and bou[gh]t our veal calf of me at 6s and the bag skin [internal organs], if ye calf proved well'.
25 May	John Brown	'So James Witton came and said yt John Brown had sent him for the veal calf that he had bou[gh]t of us: we gave it some milk and he took it away with him: and Brown haveing killd a calf this morning, we sent Harry for the feet and trindle [tail]'.
30 June	John Brown	'Walked to Ellen Seeds' where I called and paid her 3d 2 qr for her news, had a penny pot of ale and bou[gh]t a hinder quarter of a lamb of John Brown at 1s 2d and pay him and her for the ale'. [Later in the day on his way back from Preston] 'had a pint at Ellen Seeds' where he [Brown] bro[ugh]t me a leg of lamb instead of the quarter I had bou[gh]t and payd for. I [was] owed 7d. I was so displeased that he had cut the loin and sold it, I would neither have the leg nor the 7d, but left 'em all. [Brown came the following day to apologise to Walkden.]
28 July	In Preston	'Then I bou[gh]t beef, paid 1s 2d; a houghle [a shank of meat, esp. beef], payd 7d for it'.
4 August	In Preston	'Then we bought bieff in ye Shambles, cost 3s 10d'.
9 August	John Brown	'John Brown having killed a cush [perhaps a bullock], and we haveing ye tripe, my love and Margaret fetchted it home'.
8 Sept	In Preston	'...bou[gh]t near 8 pounds of onions cost 4d and 6 pounds of bieff cost 10d 2 qrs...'.

1733		
13 Sept	John Brown	'My love and Margaret went to John Brown's for tripes, he having killd a bieff today'.
25 Oct	John Brown	[We] 'went to John Brown's where rain falling briskly, we called and tho[ugh]t to go no further (dureing our stay I bou[gh]t the head of John Wharton's cow killed there today at, 10d). Rain ceasing, we went on to ye Rakefoot'. … [Following day] 'sent son Henry and Harry our Lad to John Brown's for ye cow head I bou[gh]t yesterday'.
22 Nov	John Brown	'John Brown haveing killed an ox today, my love got ye in meat [the offal], blood, liver, feet and tripes, and got them home: and we had half a loin of veal of him on Saturday last'.
23 Nov	John Brown	'So we designing to have some ox bieff off John Brown, I and my love went to John Brown's and lookt at ye bieff and bou[gh]t half a quarter at 11s. 6d., that is after £1 3s. per quarter, and we had also had 4 lbs of suet at 3d. per pound, came to 1s: I had not silver to pay at present but promised to pay as soon as moneys came into my hands: so put ye bief in a seck [sack] and laid it on our horse … and came direct home'.
15 Dec	John Brown	'My love told me yt John Brown had sent us word yt he had killd a cush [perhaps a bullock] and had a belly for us and that son Henry had fetchd it'.
21 Dec	Chipping	'My Love and I rid direct to Chipping … then we went to see for some mutton to buy but there was none yt was handsome but what Nicholas Bleasard had, and we tho[ugh]t it too dear. So we bou[gh]t none. …. Bou[gh]t two pieces of bieff weighed ye said 22 pounds, at 2d. bate [abatement] of 1½d. per pound it came to 3s but 3d. at 1½d. a pound: but I payd him 2s 7d which took 2d off'.
1734		
5 January	John Brown	'In the forenoon called John Brown who I payd 11s. 6d. for the half quarter of ox bieff I bou[gh]t of him, 1s for 4 pounds of [suit] [suet, bought 23 November]; 10d for the cow head [25 Oct.]; 1s for ye ox tripes, feet and liver [22 Nov.], in all 14s 4d so that the cow head and all I had of ye ox is to pay for, and no more'.
11 January	John Brown	'Then wentt with my love to John Brown's for a gang of calf feet'.

to be slaughtered. On 20 February 1733 Walkden offered to sell a calf to Brown, but Brown declined, evidently feeling that he could not realise its value. A couple of days later Brown agreed to slaughter the calf for Walkden and this was done on 23 February. Brown was given 2d and the calf's head as his fee. Virtually all the remainder of the animal was then sold amongst Walkden's neighbours for a little over 9s, the only part of the animal kept by the Walkdens for their own consumption being the stomach and offal. Some purchasers paid immediately: others had credit. One of them, James Witton, actually paid for his loin by ploughing for Walkden.[20] The carcass of the pig that was slaughtered a year later by Ellis Dilworth was treated differently. The pig was slaughtered on a Tuesday. The following day Dilworth came back and dismembered its carcass. One side was kept by Walkden: the other had been promised to Walkden's cousins, the Throops, and on the Thursday Peter and Catherine took it to Thomas Eccles' shop to have it weighed. It weighed 104 lbs which at 2d a pound came to 17s 4d. After the usual reconciliation of debts (including the purchase from Throops of a piglet), Walkden was owed 9s 10d. The rest of the animal seems to have been kept by the Walkdens. When Walkden's son Thomas passed by on 18 February, he left with the chine (the backbone and its flesh) and a few swine puddings.[21]

On occasion then Walkden could sell meat, but it was more usual to sell calves to Brown or another butcher.[22] On 15 February 1734 Brown came over to get a calf from Walkden. There was the usual settling of accounts and most of the value of the calf was in meat previously supplied to the Walkdens. The rest was kept by Brown as credit against future purchases. So no money changed hands, but Brown went off with the calf 'with my leather belt about its neck'. Later that day Harry went to Brown's and returned with the calf feet and trundle (tail). This seems typical of the meat that Walkden had from Brown. Most of it was poor cuts from veal calves, although on occasion Walkden bought veal loin, and a couple of times he was offered better cuts at a discount. So, meeting Brown in Ellen Seed's on 15 March 1733, 'he profferd me a shoulder of veal, it sticking on his hand. I bou[gh]t it of him'. On only one occasion did he buy beef from Brown. On successive days in November, Catherine bought ox offal (including the blood) and then they both went to inspect the rest of the carcass and bought beef and suet.

The impression is that Brown had a limited market and could not normally sell the carcass of a mature animal, and for that reason stuck to the slaughter of calves or veals. Perhaps his problem was, if the Walkdens are typical, that people simply did not eat enough meat to give him a sufficient turnover of carcasses.[23] On the evidence of the diary, the Walkdens were buying meat from him less than once a month.

20. *Diary*, 20, 22, 25 February, 26 March.
21. *Diary*, 12, 13, 14, 18 February 1734.
22. *Diary*, 10 May.
23. On 20 February 1733, Brown declined the offer of a calf from Walkden 'because he had bou[gh]t one last week and could not make his silver of it'. Walkden decided to have the calf slaughtered and then sold it as joints to his neighbours, *Diary*, 23 February.

Hence when the Walkdens wanted a superior quality of meat, they went to Preston and once to Chipping. The Preston purchases must be seen as the Walkdens' recklessness after the receipt of a subvention from Mr John Hargraves. On two successive Saturdays (28 July, 4 August), when they clearly felt they had money to spend, they bought beef.[24] They also bought beef on a couple of occasions in the autumn, and then they bought beef in Chipping in the days immediately before Christmas. Beef, then, was the meat of choice but was normally out of reach. Lesser cuts, such as calves' feet, offal and tripe were more usual but only eaten once a month at most. What is unknown is how much bacon the Walkdens had and ate. On one occasion they sold 6d of bacon to a neighbour to boil with hare.[25] If, however, they ate the half carcass of pig they were left with in February 1734 over the following year, then they had enough for 2 lbs per week, divided between a family of eight. Again, this suggests that the family ate meat as a fairly exceptional event: their own pork must have been almost a flavouring to a vegetable-based diet. Allowing for a few purchases which cannot be valued, the Walkdens spent no more than 25s on meat over the year. This is still more than the Latham family spent in the years when they had children at home, but is far short of some of the families discussed by Muldrew.[26] One is left to conclude that the Walkdens lived off potatoes and oats and had a plain and essentially meatless diet. The eagerness with which they bought beef when they had some money, and the purchase of beef at Christmas suggest that red meat was aspirational, that it was what they sought to have, but could rarely afford.

Clothing

In an oft-cited passage from the very end of the eighteenth century, Sir Frederick Eden drew a comparison between the clothing of the labourer in the Midland and southern counties and the labourer in the north. In the south and Midlands 'the labourer, in general, purchases a very considerable portion, of not the whole, of his cloaths, from the shop-keeper'. Near the metropolis they bought second-hand clothing. But in the north, and this applied to farmers and mechanics as well as labourers, 'almost every article of dress ... is manufactured at home, shoes and hats excepted'. The clothes they wore were made from homespun, and the yarn they sent to be woven and dyed, and then, one assumes, made up by tailors. Elsewhere Eden shifted his ground and acknowledged that northerners increasingly bought shop textiles, but he was adamant that 'within these twenty years, a coat bought

---

24. There is the possibility that some of this meat was for harvest workers, but Walkden tells us that he paid his workers 1s for two days and it seems that they ate at his expense on the first but not the second day of shearing. *Diary*, 9–10 August.
25. *Diary*, 23, 31 January 1734.
26. Gritt, 'Latham', Table 4.3. C. Muldrew, *Food, energy and the creation of industriousness. Work and material culture in agrarian England, 1550–1780* (Cambridge, 2011), pp. 83–100.

at a shop was considered a mark of extravagance and pride, if the buyer was not possessed of an independent fortune'.[27]

There is nothing in the Walkden diary to confirm Eden, and quite a lot to contradict him. The Walkden household spun – or rather the woman and Harry the lad did in circumstances which we will discuss later – but they did not wear homespun garments. Nor did Walkden weave, although his elder son had left home to be a check weaver.[28] One might suppose that it was the contributions from the nonconformist supporters that made it unnecessary for Walkden to weave, but equally we have no evidence elsewhere in the diary that Walkden's neighbours wove.

Walkden gives the impression of being a little vain about his clothing, but he was also willing to have a second-hand coat remodelled for him.[29] This may have come about unintentionally. Walkden was very much involved with the winding up of the estate of Richard Parker. He read Richard's will to his widow, was one of the inventory-takers and took the note of purchasers and prices at the sale of his effects. Parkers' executor had originally said that his clothes should be given to his relatives, but at least some came up at the sale. 'James Corner bought Richard's best coat at 14s 2d and it not fitting him, and he lacking silver to pay for it, I took it off his hand at the same price.' It may not be a coincidence that, two days after, the tailor Isaac Ireland 'came to sew for us and I spent the forenoon, most in helping my Love to loose and pick a coat I design to have turned'. The following day Isaac Ireland came again, and Catherine Walkden 'went to Thomas Eccles' shop and bought thread, silk and plush to trim up my coat with: and I gave her 2s to pay with'.[30] Later that day his daughter Mary was sent to Eccles' shop to buy buckram (stiffening for collars).

Other purchases seem to have been made by or with his wife in Preston. On 24 February 1733 she returned with a coat for Peter worth 8s. In May she told Peter 'that Mrs Symson of Preston had a good morning gown now by her, calamanco on both sides, which she would reserve for me, the price is 11s', but this was never (apparently) followed up.[31] The Walkdens had not the money at that time. But for a short period after the arrival of Mr Hargraves' benefaction, money was no object. On 28 July the Walkdens went into Preston (carrying, amongst other things, a letter of thanks to post to their benefactor), where they went to Mrs Seed's shop

27. Cited conveniently in Styles, *Dress of the people*, p. 135.
28. His indenture is quoted in full in *Diary*, 26 February 1734.
29. The circulation of second-hand clothing has been considered by B. Lemire, 'Consumerism in pre-industrial and early industrial England: the trade in secondhand clothes', *Journal of British Studies*, 27 (1988), pp. 1–24; M. Lambert, '"Cast-off wearing apparel". The consumption and distribution of second-hand clothing in northern England during the long eighteenth-century', *Textile History*, 35 (2004), pp. 1–26 and in Styles, *Dress of the people*, passim.
30. *Diary*, 6, 8, 9, 15 March 1733.
31. *Diary*, 12 May. The diary's editors gloss calamanco as 'a woollen cloth with glossy sheen on one side, chequered in the warp so that checks show on one side only'.

and bought Catherine Walkden a gown for 11s and a vest for 5s. They then bought beef and tobacco. The following Saturday they went back again and Walkden bought plush breeches for himself at Mrs Seed's for 4s while Catherine managed to buy two pairs of silk stockings for 1s 6d without her husband noticing.[32]

This implies the existence of shops selling ready-made clothes in Preston at this time. That this was so is shown by the experience of a further shopping day in the town in September when ready-made clothing was again purchased, but this time for son Henry. Starting at Mrs Seed's, Peter and Catherine bought him a pair of breeches for 2s. They then went to several shops and looked for vests for him but saw nothing they liked except a coat at 7s. They offered 6s 6d for this as they thought it too dear. But then they changed their minds, and Walkden sent his wife back with 7s to buy the coat if the shopkeeper would throw in a pair of gloves for the price. Walkden went off and bought beef and onions and retired to a pub for a drink. His wife met him there having clinched the deal, and they returned home. The clothes, happily, suited Henry well.[33]

And yet, even if ready-to-wear clothes were available in Preston, the Walkdens still spent a great deal of time having a tailor in the house. The usual tailor, who we have already mentioned, was a man called Isaac Ireland, although a second tailor named Robert Standen was sometimes employed as well. By my calculation, they were paid for 33 days' work in the year from February 1732, which raises the question of what they did. To answer this, we again have to confront the essential weakness of the diary, that is that Walkden is only really interested in himself. He, therefore, says that Ireland or Standen or both were in the house, 'sewing for us', and he records paying their wages, but on only three occasions does he say what they were sewing – once when Ireland remade the coat which, most likely, Walkden had bought at Parker's sale, once when he was making a riding coat for Henry and then, at the end of October, Ireland spent two days on a waistcoat for Walkden.[34] And so we come to the entirely negative conclusion that whatever the tailors were doing, it was not making clothes for Peter Walkden.

One might hope for an alternative route to answer the question of what the tailors did through the cloth that they were using. But Walkden rarely acknowledges the purchase of cloth. He had three yards of checks from his son Thomas for which he paid 2s 6d.[35] In June he went round Preston with a sample of 'stampt linen' looking for something to match it, and finally found something like it at Mr Southcoat's shop where he bought half a yard for 1s 1d.[36] But he does

32. *Diary*, 28 July, 4 August.
33. *Diary*, 8 September. It seems likely that this followed on the receipt of another grant from Mr Hargraves (27 August). Catherine Walkden had taken her step-son John into Preston the previous February to buy him shifts and a coat before he started with a new master. *Diary*, 2 February 1733.
34. *Diary*, 30–31 October.
35. *Diary*, 12 April, 4 June, 25, 28 September.
36. *Diary*, 30 June. I take a stamped linen to be a printed linen.

not tell us who this cloth was for. He made what sounds like an impulsive buy of two yards of camlet, the remainder of a roll.[37] And just before Christmas, on a Saturday when both Walkdens travelled to Preston together, his wife wanted to buy cloth. This is what he says: 'and so my love having linen cloth to buy was short of silver, so I gave her 1s and she went off to buy cloth'.[38] The implication has to be that Catherine normally bought cloth out of her earnings – from the butter and chickens – and this was an unusual subvention from her husband. A later comment confirms this: in February Catherine bought Henry a 'shift cloth', 'but what it cost I know not'. She bought herself a pair of stockings (6d) and Peter a pair of gloves (8d).[39] Hence our conclusion must be that the clothing of the younger children – and Catherine herself – was largely done at her cost, from her earnings, and the diary gives us a far from complete view of this aspect of the household's finances.

As a result, the diary tells us less than we might have wished. When he had money, Peter Walkden dipped into the ready-made clothes sector represented by Preston's shops. But he also had clothes made by jobbing tailors who worked in his house, and it seems likely that these tailors also ran up the clothes of the younger family members – and his wife. Peter was not above buying clothes second-hand and having them altered. In terms of fabrics though, we can say with confidence that the Walkdens were not using home-woven cloth, and yet it is a further lacunae in the diary that we do not really know where they procured their cloth. What we can infer is that its purchase was a part of Catherine's sphere.

Farm sales and other goods

So far we have found little sign of the Walkdens partaking of the world of new consumables. Here we find them involved in the worlds of old and second-hand goods. One of the features of the diary is the frequency with which both Peter and Catherine, sometimes together, attended farm sales, either sales prompted by the decease of the former owner or the end of his tenancy. As an example of the former we have already noted the purchase of a coat at Richard Parker's posthumous sale. The sales that the Walkdens attended and their purchases in the 14 months of the diary are given in Table 12.2.

Peter and his wife used farm sales as an opportunity to buy household items, a chair, a coup chair and its cushion,[40] bedstocks, on two occasions blankets, and kitchen and dairy equipment. Peter Walkden looked to buy pieces of farm equipment including a harrow, a wheelbarrow, a winnowing sheet, cow seals.[41]

---

37. *Diary*, 8 December. Camlet is a fine waterproof cloth, a wool and silk or wool and goat's hair mix.
38. *Diary*, 22 December.
39. *Diary*, 23 February 1734.
40. This may not have been in good condition: Walkden spent a morning 'arming it', *Diary*, 16 April.
41. Cow seals are 'ropes or chains with which to bind cattle in their stalls'. *Diary*, note to 5 October 1733.

Table 12.2 *Sales attended by Peter Walkden (PW) and Catherine Walkden (CW) in 1733–4.*

1733			
20 February	Jane Wawne	PW	An hour glass (7d); a chair (9d); three boards (1s); an aukendah (7d); old dishboard (2d).
6 March	Richard Parker	CW	A tub (2½d); a desk (6d)
		PW	A trial [sledge] (1s); two pieces pf ashwood (2d); two ladders (1s 3d); a hammer (2d)
30 March	Edmund Eccles	CW	Coup chair and cushion (2s 2d); a blanket (1s)
		PW	Wheelbarrow (1s 2d); harrow (3s 1d); swingletree single (2½d); a window [winnowing] sheet, 2s 6d; horse £6 6s.
2 May	Anne Dilworth	CW	Wool wheel and spindle (11d); a blanket (10d); a gallon (9½d)
5 October	Sail at Pail Farm	PW	Five cow seals (6½d)
25 October	Henry Wadacres	PW	10 lambs (35s)
1 November	Ann Bowrne	CW	Chair and boards (10d); bedstocks (1s 6d)
1734			
24 January	Richard Ratcliff	PW	'Thinking to have bou[gh]t a neckcollar for our horse and a calf piggen [a small wooden bucket] but ye collars were sold and the wood vessel they would sell none: however, I bou[gh]t a seck [sack] at 16d, a trail at 1s 5d and a plow at 1s, in all I wared 3s 9d'.
1 February	Daniel Slater	CW	A cheesevat (5d) and a baking skep [a bowl-shaped vessel with a handle] (1s)
7 March	Mr Phisick		'They sold no household goods that we had occasion to buy'.

He also bought ten lambs at one sale and a horse at another. Catherine, in what may have been the single most significant purchase, bought a wool wheel and spindle (11d) from the effects of Anne Dilworth. Now in this light, sales were an effective way of circulating relatively inexpensive household effects. They also allowed farmers like Walkden the opportunity to build up their stock of tools and secure larger pieces of farm equipment (all the time, of course, denuding the farm from whence they came of its economic functionality). The Walkdens did not buy new and, in terms of furnishings, fashionably: they bought second-hand, perhaps third- or fourth-hand goods.

Now this is perhaps seen in one of the most remarkable sections of the diary in which Walkden counselled his elder son. In April 1733 Thomas, who had married a fortnight earlier, came to see his father and step-mother.

> [H]e told us he wanted 50s to borrow to buy goods with to begin house with: I dissuaded him from borrowing moneys, counselled him to bring his mind to his condition and begin low, and labour hard, and be careful of what he got, and buy goods as he grew able: and I promised to give him bedstocks and chaff bed and what goods I could conveniently spare and would acquaint his uncle and aunts in Dent with his state and circumstances, but did not think they would lend him silver.[42]

On 5 May Walkden sent a cart load of household goods to his son in Blackburn: bedstocks, a bed, a bolster, a rug, an oak table, four chairs and a buffet covered with leather, and a fire iron. The circulation of second-hand goods was therefore also intergenerational: the Walkdens bought the goods of the elderly and recently deceased; some of them they passed to their own children to help them establish themselves in married life. We should not be so much surprised by this as simply grateful that for once we can see these circulations of goods.[43]

42. *Diary*, 12 April.
43. These events conform to the much more permissive pattern of marriage identified (for a slightly later period) by Emma Griffin. Thomas Walkden married at a young age (he was twenty) having served an apprenticeship for three years and one month, but without going through any process of saving or accumulation and, it would seem, without having anywhere to live with his new wife (*Diary*, p. xviii. The apprenticeship indenture is copied into the diary, 26 February 1734). There is no sign that his father had been forewarned of his marriage (or attended his marriage), but Thomas hoped that his maternal aunts and uncles might help him furnish a house. Thomas's first child was baptised in March 1734, so it seems unlikely that his wife was pregnant at the time of marriage or that the timing of the marriage was determined by sexual mischance. E. Griffin, 'A conundrum resolved? Rethinking courtship, marriage and population growth in eighteenth-century England', *Past and Present*, 215 (2012), pp. 125–64. She also observes that 'young marriage was also common amongst handloom weavers' so long as good wages could be earned (pp. 141–2).

Conclusion

One is left thinking that the only aspect of the new world of goods that had reached the Walkdens was Peter's smoking. And yet the Walkden household do conform to one of the characteristics of families dipping a toe into this pool: they set out to maximise their income by diversifying their economic activity. Or rather Catherine did. She developed a line in spinning jersey wool. There seem to have been a number of jersey weavers in the district – Walkden encountered them dining together at Throops. This, and Catherine's interest, may indicate a buoyant demand for jersey yarn. The purchase of a wool wheel may indicate that Catherine's mind was turning towards making some additional money this way. There are references to her going down to Fell End to deliver yarn or to collect more wool. The local entrepreneur seems to have been a man called James Haighton who was resident at Fell End. Walkden notes stopping off at his house when on the way to Preston to deliver yarn and collect more wool on the way back.[44] Catherine seems to have seen this as something more than a way of filling her hours. At the end of October she told Peter that she had found a young woman called Ellen Latham to come and work with her in spinning wool. Latham only stayed with the Walkdens for three and a half weeks before leaving abruptly after a sexually charged quarrel with Harry the lad,[45] but the intention is clear. In addition Catherine Walkden also appears to have been sub-contracting spinning to her neighbours. On 15 November she paid George Boardman for the work his wife had done for her. In short, she was developing as an entrepreneur in her own right. Harry the lad also decided that he would try his hand at spinning jersey, having been given it as a task to do on a day in September when it was too wet to work outdoors. In October he went for a pound of jersey and a pound of candles so that he could spin in the evenings on his own behalf.[46]

Now it may be argued that the discovery of jersey as a money-making venture could just as well be tied to the fact that the Walkdens were, money supplied by the nonconformist funds apart, seriously hard up in the summer of 1733.[47] On the other hand, the attitude of Harry the lad is more revealing: recognising that there was money to be made from spinning, he invested in both wool and candles to make use of the otherwise dead times of the day. It would be wrong to assume that Catherine's motivation was solely to have more money with which to enter into the new world of goods, but it must be conceded that her behaviour conforms to that postulated by De Vries, of leisure and dead time being converted to time spent earning. For all that this sort of behaviour has been theorised as

44. *Diary*, 23 February 1734.
45. Hoyle, 'World of Peter Walkden', p. 278.
46. *Diary*, 5 September, 23 October.
47. Hoyle, 'World of Peter Walkden', pp. 289–92.

an 'industrious revolution', it was a more elementary choice that women, in particular, have made in every generation, and one which Joan Thirsk would have understood well.

13

End piece

RICHARD JONES

It is commonplace to advise students that they should not rely on Wikipedia for information and to be very wary of its content. But this digital resource does have its uses. For one thing, it is instructive to discover what – indeed who – is included and by the same token what and who is not. It serves in this way as an excellent record of what and who has entered the public consciousness. That Joan Thirsk has a dedicated entry speaks volumes not only for the reach of her scholarship but also the wide appeal of the many historical themes she broached during her long career.[1] Nor does it come to pass for many historians to be depicted in the National Portrait Gallery, albeit in Joan's case as one of seven in Stephen Farthing's modernist ensemble piece 'Historians of "Past and Present"'.[2] By whatever criteria one cares to judge the quality and impact of Joan's scholarship and its reception – whether memorialised in high art or in the work of the people – one is left in no doubt that we are dealing with a pioneer who, in exploring parts of history overlooked or deemed beyond reach by others, became one of the most influential figures in her field, and who has left us an enduring intellectual legacy.

So many and varied were Joan's interests and contributions that framing any volume, and especially a short volume such as this, that seeks to reflect their full range is likely to come up short. Here we have chosen to focus on three broad groupings of people – farmers, innovators and consumers – whose lives, practices, choices and motivations we know so much more about as a consequence of her scholarship. Others have identified different trinities, as reflected in the title of a previous collection of essays inspired by her work, *People, Landscape and Alternative Agriculture*, a title like our own which sought the impossible, to respond to and encapsulate the breadth of 'Joan's world'.[3] Three-fold divisions of this kind also characterised her own thematic approach to individual subjects. Horses, for

---

1. <https://en.wikipedia.org/wiki/Joan_Thirsk>, accessed 25 January 2016.
2. National Portrait Gallery 6518.
3. R. Hoyle (ed.), *People, landscape and alternative agriculture: essays for Joan Thirsk* (Exeter, 2004).

example, were examined in the context of service, pleasure and power;[4] English rural communities were unpicked in terms of their structures, regularities and change over time;[5] casting her eye over the Channel, Joan's study of early modern agriculture in England and France was structured in terms of contacts, coincidences and comparisons;[6] forest, field, and garden were seen as the three key components of the landscape of Shakespeare's England;[7] and, latterly, food was explored through its phases, fads and fashions.[8] Yet, while such three-part divisions prove helpful to think with and within, ultimately, and in terms of characterisation, the world that Joan brought to life defies such strict reduction. Just as England is the sum of its regions that she so astutely defined and mapped, so Joan's scholarly world must be seen to be the sum of these many parts, three to the power x. Farmers, innovators and consumers belong to this world, indeed, they were integral to it, but they certainly do not exhaust its horizons.

In planning this volume, and the symposium that preceded it, we were keen to avoid simply exploring 'Joan's world' in retrospect. Many of the contributions here have necessarily gone back to her work, often with a critical eye, but they have done so in order to chart new ways forward. Some of Joan's original ideas and assumptions have been challenged, but it is perhaps telling that few have been dismissed out of hand; rather, it has been found necessary to readjust them or to shift their emphasis in the light of new evidence, new techniques, and new research questions. This is perhaps most clearly seen in those contributions that have revisited her foundational work on farming regions and those that examine her exploration of medieval common-field agriculture. Some contributors have returned to evidential bases that Joan herself exploited – such as probate records and diaries – while others have introduced new materials – such as retailers' inventories which she used sparingly, but not comprehensively – and by so doing have been able move their subjects forward significantly in new directions.

All have written in the spirit of Thirsk. Ordinary people have been foregrounded throughout, through the mark they have made on the landscape, through their own writings, and through the indirect mark they have left in the historical record in life and upon death. Whether by way of intimate biographies or seen more anonymously through the effects of their collective behaviour, itself the cumulative result of thousands of individual initiatives and careful decision-

---

4.   J. Thirsk, *Horses in early modern England: for service, for pleasure, for power* (Reading, 1978).

5.   J. Thirsk, 'English rural communities: structures, regularities and change in the sixteenth and seventeenth centuries', in B. Short (ed.), *The English rural community: image and analysis* (Cambridge, 1992).

6.   J. Thirsk, 'Agriculture in England and France from 1600 to 1800: contacts, coincidences, and comparisons', *Histoire, Economie et Société*, 18 (1999), pp. 5–23.

7.   J. Thirsk, 'Forest, field, and garden: landscapes and economies in Shakespeare's England', in J. Andrews (ed.), *William Shakespeare: his world, his work, his influence*, 1 (New York, 1985).

8.   J. Thirsk, *Food in early modern England: phases, fads, fashions 1500–1760* (London, 2007).

making, their story emerges clearly from the contributions presented here. Seen at times as followers, responding to the prevailing circumstances they found, and the opportunities these provided or the limitations they imposed, at others these 'ordinary' folk are revealed as leading agents responsible for extraordinary and often irreversible change. Whether as farmers or innovators or consumers – and of course these groupings are by no means mutually exclusive – we see how and in what ways English society, its economy, and its landscape were shaped at their hands. As the contributors to this volume have demonstrated, Joan's world is an expanding one. It might be confidently predicted that it will continue to grow as new generations of scholars, inspired by her writings, are encouraged to find interest and value in the study of the mundane and the quotidian and seek out innovative ways to bring the everyday to life. By so doing our understanding of England's past will be deeply enriched and humanised.

Index

accounts 6, 64, 96, 115, 127, 136, 137, 139, 143, 148
Ackroyd (surname) 13, 15
Adeney (Shrops.) 55
agents 24, 29
Agricultural History Society 7
aiglets 113
alehouses 141, 143, 145
alternative agriculture 8, 53
Alvington (Norf.) 70, 74
amercements 72
Amesbury (Hants.) 31
Anglo-Saxon 36, 39, 41, 42, 44
apples 58
aquifers 48
arable 24, 25, 26, 35, 36, 37, 38, 39, 40, 42, 43, 44, 45, 46, 47, 54, 55, 59, 62, 66, 67, 71, 84, 129
architecture 67
Arnfield, Robert 133
Ashbourne (Derbys.) 136
Ashton-in-Makerfield (Ches.) 100
assarting 38
Aston (Shrops.) 61
attorneys 90
Auxiliary Territorial Service 2

Babergh Hundred (Suff.) 82, 83, 85
Backhouse, James 111, 113, 114, 117, 118, 119, 120, 121, 122
bacon 149
Bacon, John 70, 71

bakehouses 135
Baker, William 69
bakers 130, 135, 138
Bakestone Clough (Lancs.) 134
bakestones 133–4, 135, 136, 138
baking 131, 133–4, 135
baptism registers 12
barbers 90, 91
barley 25–6, 59, 60, 126–31
barm 97, 132
Barnsley (Yorks.) 16
Barraclough (surname) 15
Baschurch (Shrops.) 61
Bawtry (Yorks.) 129
Beardsell (surname) 15
bed chambers 93
Bedford, Thomas 133
Bedfordshire 44, 115
beds 83, 111, 152, 153, 154
beef 146–7, 148, 149, 151
beer 130, 138
Bell, Miss 1
belts 107, 118, 120, 148
bibles 67, 93
Birley, John 137
Birmingham (W. Mids.) 6, 11
Blackburn (Lancs.) 154
Black Country 11
blacksmiths 59
blankets 83, 152, 153
Bleasard, Nicholas 147
Blease, Thomas 100

Garbet, Samuel 53, 57, 61
Gell, John 129
gender 64, 79, 80
genetics 13–15
Genoa 111, 112
gentry 6, 13, 56, 57, 69, 72, 92, 92, 99, 100,
    114, 136, 137
geology 21, 48, 138, *see also* chalk(lands),
    clay(lands), gritstone, limestone,
    sandstone
Germany 24, 36, 39, 109, 112, 121
girdles 107, 118, 120
Glossop (Derbys.) 16, 134
Gloucestershire 39
gloves 93, 107, 118, 151, 152
Good Sands district (Norf.) 71
Goose, Thomas 73
gossiping 98
Gough, Richard 11, 60
Gould, Joseph 132, 135
gowns 82, 107, 151
grain 32, 125, 126, 127–8, 135
Grantham (Lincs.) 1
grass 53, 59, 63
graziers 24, 52, 73
grazing 35, 38, 39, 42, 43, 45, 53, 55, 57, 60,
    61, 69, 70, 71, 74, 75
Great Budworth (Ches.) 93, 101
Great Neston (Ches.) 92
'Great Re-planning' 41
greens 43
Greenwood (surname) 15
Grimmingham (Norf.) 68, 69, 70, 71–2, 73
gritstone 129, 137
groceries 90, 94, 95, 96, 101
grocers 90, 91, 92, 94, 95, 96, 97, 98, 99, 100,
    101, 105, 112, 113, 117, 118, 120, 121, 122, 123
Gryme, Thomas 68
guilds 81
gunpowder 93
gun shot 93
Gurnell, Richard 111, 122

haberdashers 114, 115
haberdashery 93, 94, 101, 141
Haddon Hall (Derbys.) 136
Haighton, James 155
Halifax (Yorks.) 13, 15
Hallamshire 12, 13, 16
Hamburg 109
Hamer (surname) 15
hamlets 36–8, 41, 55, 141
hammers 153
Hampshire 31, 123
handkerchiefs 113
Hansen, Iris 1
hardwaremen 91
hares 149
Hargraves, John 149
Harris, Thomas 109, 114, 115, 122
Harrison, William 130
harrows 152
harvest 37, 38, 48, 69, 70, 71, 74,
Hatcher family 6
Hatfield (Herts.) 86
hats 107, 112, 118–20, 149
havercakes 131–2
hawkers 90, 92
hawking 71
Hawkins, Richard 112, 122
Hawling (Gloucs.) 39
hay 53, 60, 98, 99
Haynes, John 85
Heald, Roger 95
hearth tax 12, 13
heathland 52, 53, 54, 55, 57, 58, 61, 62, 71
hedges 65, 66, 74, 136
heifers 57
hemp 58, 82, 109, 111
Herefordshire 52, 59
Hertfordshire 21
Hey (surname) 15–16
Heydon 69
Hickling (Norf.) 67, 72, 73, 74
hidation 44